BHAVA
RATNAKARA

(A Mine of Astrological Gems)
English translation with original slokas in Devnagari

BANGALORE VENKATA RAMAN
Editor, THE ASTROLOGICAL MAGAZINE

UBS Publishers' Distributors Pvt. Ltd.
New Delhi ● Bangalore ● Chennai
Kolkata ● Patna

UBS Publishers' Distributors Pvt. Ltd.

5 Ansari Road, **New Delhi**-110 002
Phones: 011-23273601, 23266646 • Fax: 23276593, 23274261
E-mail: ubspd@ubspd.com

10 First Main Road, Gandhi Nagar, **Bangalore**-560 009
Phones: 080-2253903, 2263901, 2263902 • Fax: 2263904
E-mail: ubspdbng@eth.net

60, Nelson Manickam, Aminjikarai, **Chennai**-600 029
Phones: 044-23746222, 23746251-2 • Fax: 23746287
E-mail: ubspd@che.ubspd.com

8/1-B, Chowringhee Lane, **Kolkata**-700 016
Phones: 033-22521821, 22522910, 22529473 • Fax: 22523027
E-mail: ubspdcal@cal.vsnl.net.in

5 A, Rajendra Nagar, **Patna**-800 016
Phones: 0612-2672856, 2673973, 2686170 • Fax: 2686169
E-mail: ubspdpat1@sancharnet.in

Distributors for Western India:
M/s Preface Books
Unit No. 223 (2nd floor), Cama Industrial Estate,
Sun Mill Compound, Lower Parel (W), **Mumbai**-400 013
Phone: 022-24988054 • Telefax: 022-24988048
E-mail: Preface@prefacebooks.com

Visit us at www.ubspd.com & www.gobookshopping.com

© Mrs. Rajeswari Raman

Eighth Edition	1992
First Reprint	1993
Fifth Reprint	1997
Sixth Reprint	1998
Seventh Reprint	2000
Eighth Reprint	2001
Ninth Reprint	2003

Printed at Taj Press, New Delhi

PREFACE TO TENTH EDITION

Though the ninth edition went out of print almost immediately after its the publication, of the tenth edition had to be delayed due to my other heavy lecture and research preoccupations.

It is hoped that BHAVARTHA RATNAKARA will be of great use to all lovers of astrology, amateurs and professionals, and that it will be received with as much enthusiasm by my esteemed readers as they have shown in regard to my other books.

Thanks are due to UBS Publishers' Distributors Ltd., New Delhi, for having brought out this edition attractively.

B.V. RAMAN

Bangalore-560 020
1st February, 1992

PREFACE TO FIRST EDITION

—Celestial light

Shine inward, and the mind through all her powers
Irradiate ; there plant eyes, all mist from thence
Purge and disperse that I may see and tell
Of things invisible to mortal sight.

—MILTON

Astrology holds a prominent place in the life of every Indian. No important work is done or activity undertaken without first consulting the horoscope. When such is the case it behoves on every thinking individual to maintain the dignity and purity of the science by insisting on the necessity of a systematic study of the subject on rational and approved lines. Such a study is possible only when standard books are published. In the present day, the subject is so mishandled and misused by ignorant and ill-informed astrologers that each Tom, Dick and Harry calls himself an astrologei and some of the credulous public fall an easy prey to the snares set up by such quacks. The educated public will do well to study the general principles of the sciences so that if at all they wish to consult an astrologer, such knowledge might guide them to select the right sort of person. It is with a view to enabling the educated public to have an insight into the general principles of astrology that this translation is presented. BHAVÁRTHA RATNAKARA is a short treatise on astrology, composed by Sri Ramanuja and the way the different principles are presented by the author will not fail to make a powerful impression on the minds of the readers.

I have not simply given the translation leaving the readers to seek their own explanations of difficult principles and combinations. I have tried to explain the difficulties as best as I could by way of notes in appropriate places and by way of examples where such examples are needed. I am sure this work will be liked by my readers just as all my other books have been liked and appreciated by them.

BANGALORE   **B. V. RAMAN**
4-3-1944

INTRODUCTION

BHAVARTHA RATNAKARA is a treatise on astrology said to have been written by Sri Ramanujacharya and it deals with the subject in a masterly way. The translation, notes and examples, I have given in these pages, will speak for themselves. Several books have been written by me on astrology —some of them compilations and some of them products of my researches in the field of practical astrology. I have always felt that real astrological truths lay hidden in the Sanskrit language and the only way to bring them to the notice of the general public is to render them into English and explain the principles to the best of my humble ability and experience. My grandfather late Prof. B. Suryanarain Rao has done into English some of the most important works such as *Brihat Jataka, Sarvartha Chintamani, Jaimini Sutras,* etc., and his translations have been immensely liked by the educated public not only for the clarity with which difficult Sanskrit terms have been put into simple English but also for the vast practical experience he has brought to bear upon the inimitable notes he has given. There are a number of books extant in Sanskrit on astrology and I pitched my attention on this particular book because I found that the several combinations mentioned in it are not only useful and workable in actual practice but the entire subject of astrology has been dealt with systematically and yet concisely. I had decided to bring out a translation of this book three years ago but I had to put off the decision as I wanted to test the various principles rather exhaustively by applying them to practical horoscopes before I could bring them to the notice of the public.

The difficulties of a translator are indeed many. Prof. Rao's introduction to *Sarvartha Chintamani* will make clear the pitfalls in the way of a translator. Firstly, he should be well-versed in the subject he wishes to interpret. Secondly, he should possess a good knowledge of the language into which he intends the translation to be made. Thirdly, in a subject like astrology, mere scholarship and linguistic ability alone are not sufficient to make one a successful translator. He should possess vast practical experience which would enable him to appreciate how far a given combination can be made use of to suit different nativities. Fourthly, the flexibility of the *Sanskrit* language has been a great stumbling block in the way of rightly understanding the technical terms. Take the following verse and see whether the head or the tail of it can be made out even by an expert in Sanskrit language unless he knows the key

मा मा सौ मारि रम्भ

The principles of astrology are couched in symbolic language and one not familiar with these technicalities would only get confounded. The above line gives the friendships, enmities, etc., for the Sun while a literal rendering would give a hotch-potch meaning.

Astrology is purely a technical subject and no amount of mere scholarship in English or in Sanskrit would be of any use unless one is thoroughly familiar with the important principles of the science. The translator's responsibility rests more upon conveying the spirit of the original writer than upon simply interpreting the stanzas word by word. In other words the translation must be liberal rather than literal.

Moreover, a translation devoid of suitable explanations, examples and notes will not serve the purpose for which it is intended. Translation means the interpretation put upon the author by the translator and not the original forcible expression of the author. Therefore the difficulties of a translator are real and not imaginary.

In my translation of this work I have endeavoured to be as faithful to the original as possible not losing sight of the fact that the spirit of the author should be conveyed to the readers rather than a *verbatim* rendering or word-to-word translation. Some scholars seem to believe that they will have rendered a great service to astrology if they publish literal translations of the original Sanskrit works. They would even translate the name of the author such as for instance Kesava Daivagna as Kesava the astrologer, ignoring the fact that the words Daivagna, Sastri, etc., are used as suffixes after names.

I shall now say something about the work under consideration and its author. The book is divided into 14 Tarangas or Chapters. The total number of stanzas is 384, the First Chapter being the largest containing 130 stanzas and the Fifth Chapter being the smallest containing only 8 stanzas. Almost all Sanskrit books deal with the essentials of astrology in the first Chapter while this author has consigned the elementary principles to the last one. The First Chapter begins with a delineation of the favourable and unfavourable dispositions of planets for persons born in different lagnas. The author has made some departures at certain places from the cannons of Parasari or the principles of astrology now current. For instance while dealing with Vrishabha Lagna he says that Saturn is not a yogakaraka for Taurus in spite of the fact that he owns the 9th and 10th houses. I have tried to explain such departures in the notes to the appropriate stanzas. The Second Chapter deals with *Dhana Yogas* (combinations of wealth), *Nirdhana Yogas* (combinations for poverty), *Vidya* (education) and *Bhukti* (tastes) and contains 33 stanzas. Chapter III deals with brothers (*Bhrathru*) in the course of 10 stanzas while in the Fourth Chapter gives a fairly exhaustive treatment of *Vahanabhagya Yoga* (combinations for possessing conveyances and general fortune). Incidentally, two stanzas dispose off the fifth house. The sixth house comprehending enemies and diseases (*Satruroga*) is discussed in the Fifth Chapter in the course of 8 stanzas while the 7th house forms the subject-matter of the 13 stanzas composing the Sixth Chapter. Health and longevity (*Ayurarogya*) is disposed off in the course of 13 stanzas in the Seventh Chapter while the ninth house indications going under the general term of Fortunate Combinations (*Bhagya Yoga*) are dealt with in the Eighth Chapter. The Ninth Chapter contains 29 stanzas and deals with *Raja Yoga* and *Punya Yoga*. The Tenth Chapter, devoted to *maraka* or death, gives a number of important combinations which enable one to predict the periods and sub-periods under which one's death is likely to happen. The Eleventh Chapter gives information about the results of Dasa (*Mahadasaphala*). The principles adumbrated here are no doubt consistent with the general connons of Parasari system ; but certain combinations appear to be apparently contradictory and not explainable according to the general rules of Dasa interpretation. I have found such combinations workable in the majority of cases in actual practice. To give an illustration, stanza 26 of the Eleventh Chapter suggests that one becomes timid in the course of Rahu Dasa if Mercury is in the 3rd house. What Rahu has to do with Mercury in such a combination I cannot say. The third is the house of courage and Mercury being an impotent planet, has situation in the third and indicates want of courage. But why during the Dasa of Rahu, the subject should lose courage when Mercury is in the third is not understandable. You will however find that even the most courageous person becomes somewhat timid in the Bhukti of Mercury during Rahu Dasa. This, of course, is my own observation. The Twelfth Chapter deals with "Ordinary Combinations" (*Graha-samanya Yoga*) and gives combinations which would add vitality to the various bhavas and which would render the bhavas weak. The Thirteenth Chapter deals with *Malika Yogas* or combinations which would be formed by the disposition of planets in the fashion of the garland or wreath commencing from the Lagna and different houses. The last or Fourteenth Chapter gives the elements of astrology such as planetary ownerships, exaltations, friendships, enmities, etc. Thus it will be seen that the author has surveyed the entire field of *Phala-bhaga* or predictive astrology in a comprehensive and yet concise manner, his treatment of certain bhavas such as the fifth house being rather meagre.

As regards the author, his parentage and his place, the only evidences available are the two stanzas following the invocation at the beginning of the book and the concluding part of each chapter from which we gather the information that he is the son of Sri Bhasyam Jagannatharya (who is highly learned in astrology, a gem among scholars and well-versed in Agamas) residing in the Mahakshetra of Mangaladri and belonging to the Bharadvaja Gotra. The name of the author is given at the end of each chapter as Sri Ramanujacharya. Ever since I translated the book in 1944, I had held the view that the author of this book Sri Ramanujacharya was none other than the great Visishtadvaita philosopher. I have now been convinced that this author is a different person. More details about the author are not forthcoming. But it is evident that he was a great scholar in astrology, Sanskrit and Vedic learning.

I have tried to be as simple and clear as possible both in my translation and explanations and I am sure readers will like the translation, especially because I have tried to incorporate into the notes the experience, humble as it may be, I have gathered both in my study and practice during the last thirty years of my labours in this field.

I have only one request to make before my readers and that is if you find any mistakes or omissions in my translation and notes and if you have any reasonable and constructive criticisms to offer, bring them to my notice and I shall rectify them in the next edition.

I shall feel myself rewarded if readers find the book interesting and instructive.

BANGALORE   **B. V. RAMAN**
10-9-1958

CONTENTS

		Page
	Preface to Tenth Edition	iii
	Preface to First Edition	v
	Introduction	vii
I	Lagna or First House	1
	Mesha or Aries	1
	Vrishabha or Taurus	13
	Mithuna or Gemini	20
	Karkataka or Cancer	24
	Simha or Leo	30
	Kanya or Virgo	33
	Thula or Libra	36
	Vrischika or Scorpio	43
	Dhanus or Sagittarius	46
	Makara or Capricorn	48
	Kumbha or Aquarius	52
	Meena or Pisces	56
II	Dhana Yogas	61
	Combinations for Poverty	68
	Education	73
	Tastes or Flavours	81
III	Brothers	87
IV	Conveyances and Fortune	92
V	Enemies and Diseases	102
VI	Seventh House Indications	107
VII	Health and Longevity	112
VIII	Fortunate Combinations	120

IX	Raja Yogas	—	131
X	Combinations for Dips in Sacred Waters	—	146
XI	Combination for Death	—	150
XII	Results of Dasas	—	159
XIII	Ordinary Combination	—	172
XIV	Graha Malika Yogas	—	180
XV	Planetary Rulerships, etc.	—	193
	Index of Technical Terms		201

॥ श्रीमद्रामानुजाय नमः ॥

ज्येतिःशास्त्र भावार्थरत्नाकरः ।

अथ लग्नतरंगः ।

CHAPTER I
LAGNA OR FIRST HOUSE

मेषलग्न विचारः ।

MESHA LAGNA

मेषलग्ने तु जातस्य राजयोगोऽपि लभ्यते ।
चतुर्थपञ्चमाधीश सम्बन्धेन न संशयः ॥ १ ॥

Stanza 1.—For a person born in Mesha Lagna, Raja Yoga will undoubtedly result by the combination of the Sun and the Moon.

मेषलग्ने तु जातस्य धनसप्तमनायकः ।
शुक्रः करोति निधनमिति ज्योतिषकोविदुः ॥ २ ॥

Stanza 2.—Astrologers opine that for a person born in Mesha Lagna, Venus, lord of the 2nd and 7th, will become a maraka.

मेषलग्ने तु जातस्य भाग्यान्त्यस्थाननायकः ।
देवेन्द्रपूज्यो राज्यस्थ सभवेन्मारकः स्मृतः ॥ ३ ॥

Stanza 3.—For a Mesha Lagna person, Jupiter, lord of the 9th and the 12th, becomes a maraka if he occupies the 10th house.

मेषलग्ने तु जातस्य राजयोगो न लभ्यते ।

भाग्यराज्येश संबन्धमात्रेणहि न संशयः   ॥ ४ ॥

Stanza 4.—For a person born in Mesha Lagna
the mere combination of the lords of the 9th and the
10th, *viz.*, Jupiter and Saturn does not result in Rajayoga : This is certain.

NOTES

The author's treatment of the subject is quite comprehensive, interesting and unique. The first four stanzas make clear
the following points in respect of persons born in Mesha
Lagna :—

1. Rajayoga is caused by the mere combination of the
lords of the 4th and the 5th, *viz.*, the Moon and the Sun.

The nature of the Rajayoga, the extent of its influence and
other similar details are not elaborated by the author so that
much skill and experience are necessary on the part of the
reader who wishes to apply the principles to actual horoscopes.

2. Venus lord of the 2nd and 7th becomes a maraka.

Parasara says that because Venus happens to be the lord
of the 2nd and 7th he cannot himself become capable of inflicting death but can become a maraka only when he is in
conjunction with other marakas such as Mercury and Saturn as
Keraleeya also gives expression to Parasara's view when it
observes thus : शुक्रस्साक्षान्नहन्तास्यादिति केरल निर्णेयः । meaning that
Venus by himself cannot become a maraka. In my humble experience I have been able to come across a number of cases in
which persons born in Mesha Lagna have died in the course of
Venus Dasa.

3. Jupiter, lord of the 9th and the 12th, can become a maraka if he occupies the 10th house.

It is not clear as to why the author inclines to the view that Jupiter can become a maraka only when he is in the 10th house. Probably the author feels that because Jupiter becomes neecha (debilitated) in the 10th from Aries, he loses all benefic influences. Parasara on the other hand says that the Sun and Jupiter are benefics for Mesha Lagna. *Keraleeya* says that Mercury and Saturn become marakas for Mesha Lagna. It will be seen that an examination of a number of horoscopes reveals that Mercury is the determinant of death as he is lord of the 3rd and the 6th.

Chart No. 1. — *Born 5-3-1898 at about 9 a.m. (L.M.T.) Lat. 13° N. ; Long. 77° 35' E.*

	Lagna					Sun	Jupiter Venus
Mercury Sun Venus	RASI		Ketu Moon	Merc. Rahu	NAVAMSA		Lagna
Mars Rahu				Sat.			Mars Ketu
	Saturn		Jupit.		Moon		

Balance of Saturn's Dasa at birth :   years 2-3-19.

In *Chart No. 1,* death occurred in the 20th year of the native, in the sub-period of Saturn in the major period of Mercury. Mercury's power to kill has been fortified by his conjunction with Venus.

4. The mere combination of Jupiter and Saturn, lords of the 9th and the 10th, does not result in a Rajayoga.

This view is also supported by the great Parasara when he says that good will not be produced when Jupiter and Saturn are in conjunction.

न शुभ्रू योगमाक्षेण प्रवदेत् शनिजीवियोः ।

Chart No. 2.— *Born 13-10-1860 at about 7 p.m. L.M.T. Lat. 13° N ; Long. 77° 35' E.*

	Lagna			Rahu	Jupiter	Mars Moon
			Ketu	Merc.		
Mars Rahu	RASI		Jupit. Sat Venus		NAVAMSA	Venus Saturn
	Mercury	Sun Moon			Lagna	Ketu Sun

Balance of Moon's Dasa at birth :   years 6-1-28.

For Mesha Lagna though Saturn is lord of the 10th, he stands blemished because he is also the 11th lord. The evil is strong enough to vitiate Jupiter, the 9th lord when he happens to be associated with the 11th lord. Hence, the association of Saturn with Jupiter will not confer any yoga.

In *Chart No. 2*, the native lost his appointment in Jupiter Dasa Saturn Bhukti though both the lords are placed in the 5th house aspected by exalted Mars. However, in Mercury's sub-period, the position was regained while death also took place at the end of Mercury.

मेषलग्ने तु जातस्य स्फोट शस्त्रवणादिजम् ।
भयमस्ति च जगुः प्रायशो गणिकोत्तमाः ॥ ५ ॥

Stanza 5.—A person born when Mesha is rising will have fear from smallpox, weapons and wounds. So say the learned (in astrology).

षष्ठभाष्टमनाथेन युतो भूमिसुतो यदि ।
तद्दशान्तर्देशाकाले निधनम् मूर्ध्न कृन्तनम् ॥ ६ ॥

Stanza 6.—If Mars is in conjunction with the 6th and 8th lords, death occurs in the course of his Dasa and Bhukti by diseases pertaining to the head.

मेषे जातस्य धनपो व्ययस्थोऽपि कविश्शुभः ।
इतरर्क्षे तु जातस्य व्ययस्थ धनपोऽशुभः ॥ ७ ॥

Stanza 7.—For one born in Mesha, if the lord of the 2nd is in the 12th, he becomes good For those born in other lagnas the 2nd lord does not become good if he is placed in the 12th.

मेषे जातस्य भौमस्तु शुक्रेण सहितो यदि ।
योगदो भाविता भूयो मारकोऽपि भवेदसौ ॥ ८ ॥

Stanza 8.—For one born in Mesha Lagna Mars no doubt becomes a maraka if he is in conjunction with Venus, but still he will be capable of causing yoga also.

मेषे जातस्य भौमस्तु गुरुशुक्रसमन्वित: ।
द्वितीये यदि विधेत योगदो भवति ध्रुवम्   ॥ ९ ॥

Stanza 9.—For a person born in Mesha Lagna, Mars will certainly become a "Yogakaraka" (conferrer of fame) if he occupies the 2nd house with Jupiter and Venus.

मेषे जातस्य भौमस्तु गुरुशुक्रसमन्वित: ।
तृतीयस्थो यदि भवेद्वैव योगप्रदो भवेत्   ॥ १० ॥

Stanza 10.—For one born in Mesha Lagna, Mars does not produce any Yoga if he occupies the 3rd house with Jupiter and Venus.

मेषे जातस्य भौमस्तु गुरुणा च समन्वित: ।
चतुर्थस्थो यदि भवेद्योगदो भवति ध्रुवम्   ॥ ११ ॥

Stanza 11.—Mars will surely become a Yoga karaka for one who takes his birth in Mesha Lagna, if he is in the 4th house combined with Jupiter.

मेषे जातस्य हि कुज: पञ्चमस्थो भवेद्यदि ।
कुजदायि च संप्राप्ते योगदश्च भवेद्ध्रुवम्   ॥ १२ ॥

Stanza 12.—For a person born in Mesha Lagna, Mars in the 5th house surely causes Yoga in the course of his own Dasa.

NOTES

In the above 8 stanzas the author explains the various combinations which render Mars the lord of Lagna (*a*) capable of inflicting death and (*b*) capable of conferring yoga or fame. Summarising the above we find that :

1. Death occurs in the Dasa of Mars by diseases pertaining to the head if Mars is associated with the 6th and 8th lords. It is not clear as to what the author means when he refers to Mars being in association with 8th lord. *"Shashtabhashtama-nathena Yutho Bhumi Sutho Yadi"*. Mars is himself the 8th lord for Mesha Lagna. Consequently the 6th stanza should be taken to mean that when Mars conjoins the 6th lord, death will be caused in his Dasa. This combination is perfectly understandable because, Mars though Lagnadhipati can become a maraka when he is in conjunction with the 6th lord (Mercury) who is also the lord of the 3rd,

2. Stanza 8 says that Mars becomes a maraka, if he is in conjunction with Venus. But this does not prevent Mars from conferring Yoga also. Chart No. 2 given above reveals that Mercury did not only give rise to good results during his Bhukti but inflicted death also. Similarly, as Lagnadhipati Mars can confer beneficial results while as lord of the 8th in conjunction with lord of the 7th he can cause death also. The way the various principles are enumerated clearly reveals the author's profound knowledge of the various technicalities of the astrological science.

3. Stanza 9 says that Mars can become Yogakaraka if he is in the 2nd with Jupiter and Venus, while the 10th stanza says that the above yoga gets cancelled if the combination occurs in the 3rd house. Venus is lord of the 2nd while Jupiter is lord

of the 9th.   Mars is lord of Lagna. This combination of the lords of Lagna, 2nd and 9th is certainly indicative of immense wealth and therefore Mars becomes a Yogakaraka. When this combination occurs in the 3rd house the potency is lost. It is also found from experience that during the Dasas of Mars, Jupiter and Venus, one suffers considerably from debts, enemies, litigation, loss of honour, misunderstandings, mental worry and diseases.

4. When Mars is in the 4th (Cancer) with Jupiter the former becomes quite capable of conferring Yoga. If in addition to Mars being in Cancer with Jupiter, the Moon is also there and if Mars is in the constellation of Aslesha and Jupiter and the Moon are in Pushyami, then the sub-period of the Moon in Mars Dasa and *vice versa*, and the sub-period of the Moon in Jupiter Dasa and *vice versa* will confer Rajayoga results. There will be access to wealth, lands, houses, valuable acquaintances, realisation of ambitions, honour from rulers, getting back the amounts lent, auspicious celebrations, access to power and similar favourable happenings. Between the Dasas of Moon and Mars, if the Moon is weak, *i.e.*, waning, then the above results will be conferred during Mars Dasa. If the Moon is more powerful, then the results will happen in Moon's Dasa. Between Moon and Jupiter, the latter would definitely be more favourable.

When Mars is in the 4th for a person born in Aries, the planet becomes debilitated. If Jupiter is in Cancer, where he will be exalted, the Neecha effect of Mars is cancelled with the result, Lagnadhipati is subject to a distinct Neechabhanga Rajayoga.

In all these cases Mars seems to confer more of fame than of material possessions or wealth. Humble as my experienc has been, I have always found Mars making the native *famous* rather than *rich*.

5. According to stanza 12 Mars confers fame in his Dasa if he is the 5th.

The 5th is Leo or Simha—a friendly sign. Lagnadhipati in the 5th is always held to be good, though Parasara and Lomasa say that the native will not have much happiness from children and that the first child does not live. *"Lagnese Pancha-me Manee Sutasowkhyam cha Madhyamam Pradhamapathya Nasasyad Krodhi Rajapravesah".*

Mars may become a Yogakaraka but may render the native unhappy in respect of children.

6. Stanza 7 reveals that only in regard to Mesha Lagna lord of the 2nd in the 12th is good. For other lagnas such a disposition of the 2nd lord renders him evil.

This is a important principle worth noting and its rationale is perfectly understandable. Lord of the 2nd from Mesha is Venus ; when he is in the 12th or Pisces, he gets exalted and thereby the 2nd lord becomes strong.

मेषे जातस्य हि गुरुर्लाभस्थान स्थितो भवेत् ।
गुरोर्देशायाम् संप्रप्तावववयोगो भवेद्भुवम् ॥ १३ ॥

Stazna 13.—For a person born in Aries, Jupiter in the 11th house cannot give rise to any Yoga during his Dasa.

मेषे जातस्य पष्ठे तु झुभमौमौ स्थितौ यदि ।
तयोर्देशायां संप्राप्तौ व्रणस्फोटादि रोगदौ ॥ १४ ॥

Stanza 14.—For one born in Aries, Mercury and

Mars in the 6th will give rise to wounds, skin eruptions, smallpox and the like during their Dasas.

मेषे जातस्य भौमोऽपि सप्तमे संस्थित: कवि: ।
स्वार्जितं भाग्यमाप्नोति किंचिद्धनमुदीरितम्   ॥ १५ ॥

Stanza 15.—A person born in Mesha Lagna will possess self-earned fortune and some wealth also if Mars and Venus are in the 7th house.

मेषे जातस्य भौमस्तु अष्टमस्थो न योगद: ।
रविशुक्रसमायुक्त: स्वल्पदश्च भविष्यति   ॥ १६ ॥

Stanza 16.—For one born in Mesha Lagna Mars in the 8th house does not produce Yoga, he will how-ever confer some fame if he is in conjunction with the Sun and Venus.

भाग्यस्थौ रविभौमौ च गुरुशुक्रौ तथैव च ।
सप्तमस्थो यदि शनि: भौमो योगविशेषद: ॥ १७ ॥

Stanza 17.—For a person born in Mesha Lagna if the Sun and Mars are in the 9th as also Jupiter and Venus, and Saturn is in the 7th, then Mars produces special Yoga.

मेषलग्ने तु जातस्य लग्ने रविभृगू यदि ।
गुरुणा वीक्षितो नोच्चेच्छुक्रो योगप्रदो भवेत्   ॥ १८ ॥

Stanza 18.—For a person born in Mesha Lagna,

Venus becomes capable of giving rise to Yoga provided he is in Lagna with the Sun unaspected by Jupiter.

गुरुणा वीक्षितइशुक्रो योगदो न भवेध्रुवम् ।
गुरुणा वीक्षितस्सूर्यो योगदो भर्वति ध्रुवम्   ॥ १९ ॥

Stanza 19.—Venus aspected by Jupiter will not certainly confer any Yoga. But the Sun aspected by Jupiter becomes a Yogakaraka.

मेषलग्ने तु जातस्य रविसौम्य सितास्तथा ।
लाभस्था यदि तेषां च दशाभाग्यप्रदा स्मृता   ॥ २० ॥

Stanza 20.—For a person born in Mesha Lagna, if the Sun, Mercury and Venus are in the 11th, they will give rise to fortune during their respective Dasas.

मेष जातस्य लग्नस्थो भानुः क्कर्कटके यदि ।
चन्द्रो यदि भवेज्जातः राजयोगग् समश्नुते   ॥ २१ ॥

Stanza 21.—For a person born in Mesha, Raja-yoga is caused if the Sun is in Lagna and the Moon is in Cancer.

मेषलग्ने तु जातस्य शुक्रेज्यार्यम्णो यदि ।
राज्यस्थस्तद्दशाकाले गंगास्नानम् भविष्यति   ॥ २२ ॥

Stanza 22.—A person born in Mesha Lagna will have dips in the Ganges in the Dasas of Venus, Jupiter and the Sun if the said planets are in the 10th.

NOTES

The above stanzas are simple enough and do not call for any elaborate explanations. However, we may summarise the various principles enunciated therein so that the reader may understand them clearly.

(1) Jupiter in the 11th does not produce any Yoga in his Dasa. (2) Mars and Mercury in the 6th give rise to wounds, skin eruptions, cuts and the like in their Dasas. (3) Mars cannot produce any Yoga by himself when he is in the 8th in his own house, but can confer slight fame if he is with the Sun and Venus. (4) situation of Venus and Mars in the 7th is favourable for self-acquisition of fortune and wealth. (5) Mars causes special Yoga when the Sun and *Mars* and Jupiter and Venus are in Sagittarius and Saturn is in the 7th. (6) Venus confers *some fame* if he is in the Ascendant with the Sun unaspected by Jupiter while the Sun confers fame when he receives Jupiter's aspect.

Chart No. 3. --*Born on 9-6-1891 at Gh. 55-20, Lat. 19° N. ; Long. 72° E,*

	Lagna	Venus Sun Rahu Mercury	Mars				Rahu Jupiter
Jupiter		RASI	Moon	Merc		NAVAMSA	
			Sat.	Mars Venus			
	Ketu			Lagna	Ketu	Saturn	Sun Moon

Balance of Saturn's Dasa at birth : **years 13-10-22.**

(8) The Dasas of the Sun, Mercury and Venus will prove beneficial if the said planets are in the 11th and finally, (9) the
Sun in Ascendant and the Moon in Cancer are beneficial as
causing Rajayoga. This particular yoga appears to have been
taken from *Brihat Jataka* (XI. 2)

In *Chart No. 3,* Venus is in Lagna and is unaspected by
Jupiter. The native has risen from humble beginnings to a
fairly responsible position.

अथ वृषभलग्न विचारः ।

VRISHABHA LAGNA

वृषभजातस्य च शनिः भाग्यकर्मेश्वरोऽपि वा ।
सूर्यसोमसुताभ्याम् वा न युक्तौ नैव योगदः   ॥ १ ॥

Stanza 1.—For a person born in Vrishabha Lagna
Saturn does not become Yogakaraka in spite of his
owning the 9th and 10th houses from Lagna ; nor do the
Sun and Mercury become capable of producing Yoga
even if they join the Lagna.

वृषभर्क्षेऽपि जातस्य राज्येराहुर्यदि स्थितः ।
मकरे गुरुभौमौ वा गंगास्नानम् समश्नुते   ॥ २ ॥

Stanza 2.—A person born in Vrishabha Lagna
will have dips in Ganges if Rahu is in the 10th or Mars
and Jupiter are in Capricorn.

वृषभे जायमानस्य चतुर्थं यदि चन्द्रमाः ।
गुरुणा च बुधेनापि वीक्षितो यदि योगदः ॥ ३ ॥

Stanza 3.—For one born in Vrishabha Lagna
Moon becomes capable of producing Yoga if he occupies the 4th, aspected by Jupiter or Mercury.

वृषभे जायमानस्य कुजस्सप्तमगश्शुभः ।
लाभस्थौ भानुभाग्येशौ दीर्घायुर्योगवान् सदा ॥ ४ ॥

Stanza 4.—For a person born in Vrishabha Lagna
Mars becomes a benefic in the 7th house. Long life is
indicated if the Sun and lord of the 9th are in the 11th.

वृषभलग्ने तु जातस्य गुरोस्सोमसुतस्य च ।
संबन्धो वीक्षणम् वाऽपि विद्यते धनयोगदः ॥ ५ ॥

Stanza 5.—For one born in Vrishabha Lagna if
Jupiter and Mercury are in conjunction or in mutual
aspect Dhanayoga is caused.

वृषभे जायमानस्य गुरोस्सोमसुतस्य च ।
कुजेन सहसंबन्धो वीक्षितो वा भवेद्यदि ।
विशेष धनसंप्राप्तिम् न प्राप्नोति न संशयः ॥ ६ ॥

Stanza 6.—The Dhanayoga becomes defunct if
Jupiter and Mercury are in conjunction with or aspected by Mars.

NOTES

The great Parasara observes thus : "*Rajayogakarah Sak-
shadeka Yeva Raveh Sutha*" meaning that Saturn is the only

planet capable of producing Rajayoga for Taurus Ascendant. In the face of this assertion by no less a personage than Parasara, the author of the work observes that Saturn even though lord of the 9th and the 10th does not produce Yoga. When two great authors express two different views we have to stick to the opinions of the greater of the two, or rely upon our own experience. Parasara is undoubtedly the greatest because he is not only a Maharshi but what he says is held to be beyond question. Our author in suggesting Saturn as incapable of giving good results might have had in view reasons justifiable in their own way and he might not certainly have meant any disrespect for Parasara. When stanza 1 is clear no other meaning can be read into it than what it implies. Probably the author felt that Saturn, though he may produce Rajayoga by owning the 9th and 10th houses, might render the native unable to achieve in full measure the fruits of such Yoga because Saturn is by intrinsic nature a malefic. Prof. B. Suryanarain Rao's words are still ringing fresh in my ears when he said to me that Saturn would doubtless produce Rajayoga but he would not enable the person to consolidate his gains—political and material. Again much depends upon how Saturn is situated in the horoscope. If he is in the 10th it is a good position. If he is in the 2nd it yields destructive influences. The native earns money, fame and reputation but an outlet for the exit of all these will be present in some form or other.

In stanza 3, the Moon is said to be capable of causing Yoga if he occupies the 4th house. But according to Parasara, the Moon is evil for Taurus Ascendant. If the Moon is aspected by Jupiter a Yoga is said to result.

Combination enunciated in stanzas 5 and 6 seems to be sound and reasonable. Dhanayoga is caused by the conjunction of Jupiter and Mercury (lord of 2) and this Dhanayoga becomes defunct if Mars also joins the combination. Mars is lord of 12 (house of loss) and naturally wealth indicated will be removed by the 12th lord.

वृषमे जायमानस्य गुरुसौम्यकुजा यदि ।
परस्परयुतास्तौम्यदायस्तु ऋणयोगदः   ॥ ७ ॥

Stanza 7.--For one born in Taurus Ascendant if Jupiter, Mercury and Mars join together or aspect one another, there will be debts during Mercury's Dasa.

भौमदायस्तु धनदो गुरोर्दायस्तु मिश्रदः ।
कन्द्रस्थितस्य सौम्यस्य दायोर्योगप्रदस्स्मृतः   ॥ ८ ॥

Stanza 8.--For a person born in Taurus Ascendant, Mars Dasa will give financial prosperty and Jupiter's Dasa produces mixed results ; provided Mercury is in a Kendra, he produces Yoga in the course of his Dasa

लग्नस्थौ बुधशुक्रौ तु सप्तमस्थो गुरुर्यदि ।
बुधदायस्तु प्रबलयोगदो वृषजन्मनः   ॥ ९ ॥

Stanza 9.—For a person born in Taurus Ascendant, during Mercury Dasa powerful Yoga will be caused, if Mercury and Venus are in the Ascendant and Jupiter is in the 7th.

लग्नस्थौ कुजशुक्रौ तु मकरस्थो गुरुर्यदि ।
गुरुसौम्यदशाकाले भाग्यंस्याद् वृषजन्मनः   ॥ १० ॥

Stanza 10.—For a person born in Taurus Ascendant if Mars and Venus are in the Ascendant and Jupiter is in Capricorn the Dasas of Mercury and Jupiter will prove fortunate.

मन्दसौम्यकुजा भाग्ये राहुः कुंभगतो यदि ।
कुजराहुदशा गंगास्नानदा वृषजन्मनः ॥ ११ ॥

Stanza 11.—A person born in Taurus Ascendant will have dips in Ganges during the Dasas of Mars and Rahu if Saturn, Mercury and Mars are in the 9th and Rahu is situated in Aquarius.

चन्द्रशुक्रौ तु षष्ठस्थौ लाभे सौम्यगुरू यदि ।
गुरुदाये च संप्राप्ते धनयोग उदीरितः ॥ १२ ॥

Stanza 12.—Jupiter Dasa will cause Dhanayoga, if the Moon and Venus are in the 6th and Mercury and Jupiter are in the 11th.

शुक्रस्यदाये संप्राप्ते धनप्राबल्यमादिशेत् ।
भाग्ययोगं समाप्नोति वृषजन्म न संशयः ॥ १३ ॥

Stanza 13.—A person born in Taurus Ascendant will undoubtedly get plenty of wealth in the course of Venus Dasa; and he will also enjoy "Bhagya Yoga",

वृषमे जायमानस्य लग्ने चन्द्रस्थितो यदि ।
विशेष धनयोगं तु न प्राप्नोति जातकः   ॥ १४ ॥

Stanza 14.—One born in Taurus Ascendant will not have much Dhanayoga if the Moon is situated in Lagna.

इतरर्क्षे जायमानो भाग्यवान् भवति ध्रुवम्   ॥ १५ ॥

Stanza 15.—If birth happens in other signs (than Taurus) and the Moon is in the Ascendant then the native will certainly become fortunate.

NOTES

In these nine stanzas, the formation of Yogas by the different kinds of combinations of planets is discussed. Summarising we may observe that, with reference to Taurus Ascendant :—

(1) Mars, Jupiter and Mercury can produce Yoga (confer fame) by mutual combination and aspect. Mercury and Mars may give rise to Yoga as lords of the 5th and the 7th but how Jupiter being lord of the 8th and the 11th can form Yoga is incomprehensible. Jupiter can produce fairly good results if he is in the 10th house and not otherwise.

(2) Access to wealth in Mars Dasa, mixed results in Jupiter Dasa, and power and fame in Mercury Dasa (if Mercury is in a Kendra) may be predicted.

(3) Good results will be produced in Mercury Dasa if Mercury and Venus are in the Ascendant and Jupiter is in the 7th.

(4) Jupiter and Mercury Dasas will be fortunate if Venus and Mars are in the Ascendant and Jupiter is in Capricorn.

It will be seen in this combination that Jupiter should be in Capricorn (9th house) where he is debilitated. This debilitated effect is said to be cancelled by the disposition of Mars, Mercury and Venus in the Ascendant.

(5) There will be access to wealth in Jupiter Dasa if the Moon (lord of 3) and Venus (lord of 6) are in the 6th and Mercury and Jupiter are in the 11th.

(6) The presence of the Moon in the Ascendant deprives wealth.

Chart No. 4.—*Born on 12–1–1856 at Gh. 12–21 p.m., L.M.T. Lat. 80° N. ; Long. 84° E.*

	Moon Rahu	Ascdt.	Sat.	Jupit.		Ascdt.	Rahu
Sun Mercury Jupiter		RASI				NAVAMSA	
				Marc.			
Venus		Mars Ketu		Ketu		Moon Sun Saturn Venus Mars	

Balance of Venus Dasa at birth : years 6–11–3.

In *Chart No. 4* Jupiter is with Mercury (lord of 2 and 5) and the Sun (lord of 4) in the 10th. The Sun–Mercury combination is a distinct Rajayoga and Jupiter, probably by virtue of his connection with this Rajayoga, derived power to do good in respect of the Bhava occupied by him. The native built up his reputation in the course of Jupiter Dasa and had good earnings throughout the period. At the end of this Dasa however he fell seriously ill, and in the Bhukti of Rahu (mark Rahu is in the 12th ruling feet and aspected by Mars) two fingers in the left foot of the native were removed by a surgical operation. From the Moon, Jupiter is lord of the 9th and is in the 11th and the disposition of planets from the Moon should not be ignored when making predictions.

अथ मिथुनलग्न विचारः

MITHUNA LAGNA

तृतीयस्थौ रविबुधौ बुधदाये समागमे ।
बुधो योगप्रदस्सत्य युग्मजातस्य भाग्यदः   ॥ १ ॥

Stanza   1.-- For a person born in Gemini Ascendant, if the Sun and Mercury are placed in the 3rd house, Mercury will surely produce Yoga in his Dasa besides giving rise to beneficial results.

भृगुभौमेन्दवः खेटाः धनस्थाने स्थिता यदि ।
शुक्रदाये धनप्राप्तिं युग्मजातस्समश्नुते   ॥ २ ॥

Stanza   2.—If Venus, Mars and the Moon are in the 2nd, during Venus Dasa there will be access to wealth for a person born in Gemini Ascendant.

मिथुने जायमानस्य धरासूनुर्धने स्थितः ।
शनिचन्द्रावष्टमस्थौ शनेर्दाये समागमे   ॥ ३ ॥

Stanza 3.—For one born in Gemini Ascendant if Mars is in the 2nd and the Moon and Saturn are in the 8th, then during the Dasa of Saturn·

शनिस्तु मिश्रफलदः कुजदाये समागमे ।
धनयोगो भवत्येव जातकस्य न संशयः   ॥ ४ ॥

Stanza 4.—Saturn will give mixed results. Mars will undoubtedly give rise to Dhanayoga in his Dasa.

मिथुने जायमानस्य कुजमन्दौ द्वितीयगो ।
अष्टमस्थौ भवेदिन्दु शनिभौम दशागमे   ॥ ५ ॥

Stanza 5.—If Mars and Saturn are in the 2nd and the Moon is in the 8th, then when the Dasas of Saturn and Mars commence :—

तत्काले धनहीनस्यात्पूर्वभाग्यं विनश्यति ।
किञ्चिद्धनयुतो जातो भवेदेवं न संशयः   ॥ ६ ॥

Stanza 6.—The native loses wealth, and property will be destroyed, but still he will retain some money.

मिथुने जायमानस्य धननाथस्तु चन्द्रमाः ।
मारको न भवत्येव मानवस्य न संशयः   ॥ ७ ॥

Stanza   7.—The Moon who is the lord of the 2nd does not become a maraka for a person born in Gemini Ascendant.   This is undoubted.

मिथुने जायमानस्य कुजचन्द्रौ तु लाभगौ ।
भाग्यस्थो यदि वा मन्दो विशेष धनयोगदः   ॥ ८ ॥

Stanza   8.—A powerful Dhanayoga will be caused for a person born in Gemini Ascendant if the Moon and Mars are in the 11th and Saturn is in the 9th.

युग्मजातस्य भाग्यस्थौ गुरुमन्दौ तयोर्दशा ।
काले भवति गंगायास्नानं भवति निश्चयं   ॥ ९ ॥

Stanza   9.—The native will have dips in Ganges and other sacred rivers in the Dasas of Jupiter and Saturn provided these planets are in the 9th house.

मिथुने जायमानस्य बुधो लाभस्थितो यदि ।
ज्येष्ठभ्रातृ विरोधस्तु जातकस्य भवेध्रुवम्   ॥ १० ॥

Stanza   10.—If Mercury is in the 11th house the native will have misunderstandings with his eldest brother.

NOTES

The combinations are clear and can be easily understood by the readers.   Mars is a malefic for Gemini Ascendant but according to stanza 4 one will have access to wealth in Mars

Dasa if Mars is in the 2nd and Saturn and the Moon are in the 8th. This means that Mars will be in debilitation and also implies presence of Neechabhanga (by virtue of the Moon lord of the 2nd aspecting the 2nd as also Saturn lord of the 9th); otherwise Mars cannot give financial prosperity. Stanza 6 makes it clear that if Mars and Saturn are in the 2nd, the Moon is in the 8th, wealth will be destroyed in Mars Dasa. The differentiation in disposition for giving wealth and taking away wealth is that for the former result Saturn must be in rhe 8th with the Moon while Mars should be in the 2nd ; and for the latter the Moon must be in the 8th while Saturn and Mars must be in the 2nd. The centre of gravity is Saturn. He will destroy the indication of the 2nd if he is present there.

These are indeed unique combinations and call for much power of analysis on the part of the reader to understand their proper implication.

Chart No. 5.—*Born on 11–4–1880 at Gh. 12 after sunrise. Lat. 18° N. ; Long. 5h. 34m. E.*

Mercury Venus Jupiter Saturn	Moon Sun		Ketu Mars Ascdt.	Ketu Sat. Ascdt.	Sun		
	RASI 300—20				NAVAMSA		
							Venus
Rahu					Mars	Jupiter Mercury	Moon Rahu

Balance of Moon's Dasa at birth : years 11–6–27.

Stanza 8 says that the Moon and Mars in the 11th and Saturn in the 9th give rise to immense wealth.

In *Chart No. 5* the Moon is in the 11th. The native rose from ordinary rungs and made a lot of money. The Moon is free from any afflictions and this is a great asset. There are no fewer than 6 planets in the Ascendant and the 10th house. This indicates an active and rapidly moving mind fitted to play a mighty part.

अथ कटकलग्न विचार:

KARKATAKA LAGNA

कर्किंजातस्य च गुरुर्विशेषेण न योगद: ।
मकरे जायमानस्य बुधो योगप्रदो भवेत्   ॥ १ ॥

Stanza   1.—Jupiter does not cause any special Yoga for one born in Cancer Ascendant. But Mercury is productive of Yoga for a person born in Capricorn.

कर्कटे जायमानस्य भौमो योगप्रदो भवेत् ।
पञ्चमे वाथराज्येवा रोगदो भवति ध्रुवम्   ॥ २ ॥

Stanza   2.—Mars becomes Yogakaraka to a person born in Cancer; if he also happeens to be either in the 5th or 10th house, he becomes more powerful to confer Yoga.

कर्किजातस्य शुक्रस्तु व्ययस्थो धनगोऽपि वा ।
योगप्रदस्तु भवतिह्मन्यत्र नहि योगदः ॥ ३ ॥

Stanza 3.—Venus causes Yoga if he is placed either in the 12th or in the 2nd house ; in other places he will not produce any Yoga.

कर्किजातस्य भौमेज्य चन्द्रश्च धनगो यदि ।
रविशुक्रौ पञ्चमस्थौ धनवान् भाग्यवान् भवेत् ॥ ४ ॥

Stanza 4.—A person born in Cancer Ascendant will become wealthy and fortunate if Mars, Jupiter and the Moon are in the 2nd house and the Sun and Venus are in the 5th house.

बुधशुक्रौ पञ्चमस्थौ बुधदायें समागमे ।
कर्किजातस्य च बुधो योगदो भवति ध्रुवम् ॥ ५ ॥

Stanza 5.—For a person born in Cancer if Mercury and Venus are in the 5th, Mercury will produce Yoga in the course of his Dasa.

कर्किजातस्य लाभे तु सौम्यशुक्रेन्दवस्थिताः ।
लग्नसंस्थो यदि गुरुः राज्यस्थाने स्थितो रविः ॥ ६ ॥

Stanza 6.—If Mercury, Venus and the Moon are in the 11th house, Jupiter in the Ascendant and the Sun in the 10th :

राजा भवेत्साहसिकः गुणवान् कीर्तिवान् भवेत् ।
बृहज्जातकयोगोयं महाराजिक संज्ञिकः ॥ ७ ॥

Stanza 7.—The native will become a king who is capable, famous and of good character. This particular combination goes under the name of Maharajayoga in *Brihat Jataka.*

NOTES

Jupiter though lord of 9 for Cancer Ascendant will not produce Rajayoga while Mercury produces Rajayoga for Capricorn Ascendant. In both these cases, the planets in question own the 6th and 9th houses,—but why should Mercury cause Yoga. The explanation is simple. In respect of Mercury along with the 9th lordship, exaltation place is also combined while this is not the case in reference to Jupiter.

If you examine carefully several horoscopes of persons born in Cancer Ascendant you will invariably find that Jupiter in his Dasa has given rise to both good and bad results—bad in respect of debts, diseases and enemies. Though Jupiter may not cause Rajayoga in the strict sense, he has promoted the business and professional prospects involving the native at the same time in misunderstandings, troubles, annoyances and ill-health.

Venus in the 12th or 2nd gives rise to a benefic Yoga. Venus is lord of the 4th and the 11th and his presence in the 2nd though in an inimical house is approved by the author.

The subject of *Chart No. 6* is short, strong, nervous, extremely sensitive and dark in complexion. The native is unimaginative, miserly, mean and undignified and cautious. There are several malefic combinations in this horoscppe and we are

Chart No. 6.—*Born on 29–7–1909 at Gh. 1-15 after sunrise. Lat. 13° N. ; Long. 77° 43′ E.*

Mars	Saturn	Rahu			Saturn		Venus
		Sun Merc. Ascdt.		Moon			Rahu
RASI				NAVAMSA			
		Jupit. Venus		Ketu			
	Moon Ketu			Ascdt.	Sun	Mars Jupiter	Mercury

Balance of Mercury's Dasa at birth : years 6–61–6.

concerned with only two points, *viz* , Cancer rising as Ascendant and Venus being placed in the 2nd. The native earned fairly decently and also acquired landed properties.

रविभौमौ तु राज्यस्थौ धनवान् कर्किजातकः ।
कर्किजातस्य च गुरोर्द्रेशाकालस्तु मारकः   ॥ ८ ॥

Stanza 8.—A person born in Cancer Ascendant will become rich if the Sun and Mars are in the 10th house. Death will occur in the course of Jupiter Dasa.

कर्कटे जायमानस्य बुधशुक्रौ व्ययस्थितौ ।
शुक्रदाये च संप्राप्तो राजयोग उद्दीरितः   ॥ ९ ॥

Stanza 9.—A person born in Cancer Ascendant will enjoy Rajayoga in the course of Venus Dasa if Mercury and Venus are in the 12th house.

कर्कटे जायमानस्य चन्द्रजीवौ तु लग्नगौ ।
राजयोग इति प्रोक्तः भाग्यवान्कीर्तिमान्भवेत्   ॥ १० ॥

Stanza 10.—For a person born in Cancer the combination of the Moon and Jupiter in the Ascendant results in the Rajayoga. This makes him fortunate and famous.

कर्कटे जायमानस्य चन्द्रो लग्ने स्थितो यदि ।
मकरस्थो भवेत्सौमः राजयोग उदीरितः   ॥ ११ ॥

Stanza 11.—Rajayoga is also caused if the Moon is in the Ascendant and Mars is in Capricorn.

कर्कटे जायमानस्य लग्ने चन्द्रस्थितो यदि ।
तुलायां यदि मन्दस्तु राजयोग उदीरितः   ॥ १२ ॥

Stanza 12.—If the Moon is in the Ascendant and Saturn is in Libra, then also Rajayoga is produced.

कर्कटे जायमानस्य चन्द्रो लग्ने स्थितो यदि ।
मेषस्थितो यदि रविः राजयोग उदीरितः   ॥ १३ ॥

Stanza 13.—Rajayoga results if the Moon is in the Ascendant and the Sun is in Aries.

कर्किजातस्य लग्नस्थौ रविसौम्यौ तु सौख्यग: ।
कविल्लाभे चन्द्रभौमगुरव: संस्थिता यदि   ॥ १४ ॥

Stanza 14.—If the Sun and Mercury are in the Ascendant, Venus in the 4th, and the Moon, Mars and Jupiter are in the 11th :

रवेर्दायै तु संप्राप्ते निर्धनं योगमश्नुते ।
इतरेषां दशाकाले योगदास्तु भवन्ति हि   ॥ १५ ॥

Stanza 15.—The native loses wealth in the course of the Sun's Dasa while in the other Dasas, he will enjoy good results.

गंगास्नानं कर्किजस्य गुरुसौम्यौ तु लाभगौ ।
शनिराहू पञ्चमस्थौ राहुदाये तु सिध्यति   ॥ १६ ॥

Stanza 16.—The native will surely have dips in the Ganges in Rahu Dasa if Jupiter and Mercury are in the 11th and Saturn and Rahu are in the 5th.

NOTES

These nine stanzas give several Rajayogas and they need no explanation as the stanzas are quite simple.

अथ सिंहलग्न विचारः
SIMHA LAGNA

सिंहलग्ने तु जातस्य रविसौम्यकुजा यदि ।
परस्परेण संयुक्ता धनबाहुल्यमादिशेत्   ॥ १ ॥

Stanza 1.—For a person born in Leo Ascendant
if the Sun, Mercury and Mars are conjoined together,
good wealth is indicated.

सिंहलग्ने तु जातस्य रविजीवबुधा यदि ।
परस्परेण संयुक्ता धनबाहुल्यमादिशेत्   ॥ २ ॥

Stanza 2.—For a person born in Leo Ascendant
if the Sun, Jupiter and Mercury are combined together,
good wealth is indicated.

सिंहलग्ने तु जातस्य रविसोमसुता यदि ।
अन्योन्य संयुतौ स्यातां खल्प भाग्यमुदीरितम्   ॥ ३ ॥

Stanza 3.—If the Sun and Mercury are in conjunction, the native will enjoy some fortune.

सिंहलग्ने तु जातस्य गुरुशुक्रौ न योगदौ ।
योगभंगकरौ किंतुर्विदुर्ज्येतिषकोत्तमाः   ॥ ४ ॥

Stanza 4.—The learned in astrology say that for
a person born in Leo Ascendant, Jupiter and Venus

do not produce any Yoga. On the other hand they cause destruction of the Yoga.

सिंहलग्ने तु जातस्य तृतीयस्थो भृगुश्शुभः ।
राज्यस्थः शुक्रपापस्याब्रयोगं लभते नरः ॥ ५ ॥

Stanza 5.—For a person born in Leo Ascendant, Venus becomes a benefic in the 3rd house; he becomes a malefic in the 10th: Therefore Venus can produce no Yoga.

सिंहलग्ने तु जातस्य रविसौम्यकुजा स्थिताः ।
लग्ने बुधदशाकालः धनभाग्यबहुप्रदः ॥ ६ ॥

Stanza 6.—The subject gains much wealth and fortune in Mercury Dasa if the Sun, Mercury and Mars are in the Ascendant.

कुजमन्दौ व्ययस्थौ चेल्छार्निदाये समागमे ।
शनियोगप्रदस्सत्यं सिंहजातस्यवै ध्रुवम् ॥ ७ ॥

Stanza 7.—Saturn causes Yoga in his Dasa if Mars and Saturn are in the 12th. This is certain.

NOTES

The Sun, Mercury and Mars are said to give rise to wealth in mutual combination. The Sun is lord of the Ascendant, Mercury lord of wealth and Mars is of course Yogakaraka. Thus all the three planets have acquired some power or other to do good. Jupiter is lord of the 5th. Therefore his association is also permissible. If the Sun and Mercury are combined, some fortune is granted while Mars stepping in gives immense fortune. As Jupiter and Venus are lords of the 8th and the 3rd, their combination is not conducive to prosperity. Venus in the 3rd is good while in the 10th he is bad as he owns a kendra besides being located there. Saturn in the 12th with Mars is good. Thus it will be seen that the Sun, Mercury and Mars play an important role in case of persons born in Leo Ascendant, while other planets will be able to do some good under certain special conditions.

Chart No. 7.— *Born on 14-5-1896 at 17 Gh. after sunrise at Lat. 13° N, ; Long. 77° 35' E.*

Mars	Venus	Sun Moon Mercury			Saturn	Ascdt. Ketu
Rahu			Jupit.			Moon
	RASI			NAVAMSA		
			Ascdt. Ketu	Sun		Mercury Mars
	Saturn			Rahu	Jupiter	Venus

Balance of Moon's Dasa at birth : years 2–5–21.

In *Chart No. 7,* the Sun and Mercury are in the 10th together. The native is earning decently, but he has not saved anything.

Chart No. 8.—*Born on 28/29-8-1898 at 5-33 a.m. L.M.T. Lat. 16° 50′ N. ; Long. 75° 45′ E.*

			Mars Ketu		Moon	Ketu	Jupiter
							Ascdt.
	RASI		Sun Ascdt. Merc.		NAVAMSA		Sun
Moon							
Rahu	Saturn		Jupit Venus	Merc.	Rahu Mars Saturn		Venus

Balance of Venus Dasa at birth : years 9-8-12.

On the other hand in *Chart No. 8,* the Sun and Mercury are together in the Ascendant and the native is in very well-to-do circumstances though he had a checkered career.

अथ कन्यालग्न विचार:

KANYA LAGNA

कन्यालग्ने तु जातस्य भृगोश्चन्द्रय वा यदि ।
संबन्धो यदि विद्येत रवेर्दाये धनागमः ॥ १ ॥

Stanza 1.—For a person born in Virgo Ascendant if the Sun is related to Venus or the Moon by mutual conjunction, aspect, etc., there will be access to wealth in the course of Sun's Dasa.

NOTES

Here is a combination which suggests that a planet who is the lord of the 12th or the house of loss gives access to wealth under certain conditions. As the Sun happens to be the lord of the 12th for Virgo he cannot give independent results. He partakes of the results of the planets he is in conjunction with or aspected by. As Venus is lord of the 2nd and the 9th and the Moon is the lord of the 11th, the Sun gives results pertaining to wealth, fortune and gains. It is such combinations which are elusive in their nature and escape the notice of students of astrology.

शुक्रदाये च संप्राप्ते धनहीनो भवेन्नरः ।
चन्द्रदाये च संप्राप्ते मिश्रयोगं समश्नुते ॥ २ ॥

Stanza 2.—The person becomes bereft of wealth in Venus Dasa. Mixed results will happen in the course of Moon's Dasa.

NOTES

Here evil results are predicted in the course of Venus Dasa provided Venus is connected with the Sun by conjunction or aspect as given in the preceding stanza.

As Venus is the natural enemy of the Sun, and as the Sun becomes beneficial to produce good results, Venus probably becomes deprived of the good results he would have produced pertaining to the 2nd and 9th houses if he were not connected with the Sun either by aspect or by conjunction. The evil results ascribed for Venus Dasa should not be predicted if Venus is not subject to conjunction or aspect of the Sun.

चन्द्रशुक्रौ सप्तमथयौ लाभस्थो यदि वा गुरुः ।
मेषे रविर्गुरोर्दाये शुक्रदाये समागमे ॥ ३ ॥

Stanza 3.—A person born in Virgo, with the Moon and Venus in the 7th, Jupiter in the 11th and the Sun in Aries will, during the Dasas of Jupiter and Venus:—

चतुश्र: पञ्चमा जीवकल्त्राणि न संशय: ।
कन्यायां जायमानस्य राजतुल्यस्य कामिन: ॥ ४ ॥

Stanza 4.—Possess 4 or 5 wives who will be alive. And one born in Virgo will also possess women of high rank.

NOTES

This is a difficult combination because it says that a person born in Virgo with the Moon and Venus in the 7th, Jupiter in the 11th and the Sun in Aries, will possess 4 or 5 wives in the course of Dasas of Jupiter and Venus. The combination is indeed rare. Three planets are exalted—Venus in the 7th, the Sun in the 8th and Jupiter in the 11th. The combination can be adapted to suit modern times and conditions to the extent that a person born with planets disposed as stated above will have a romantic life.

कन्यायां जायमानस्य गुरुशुक्रौ चतुर्थगौ ।
गुरुशुक्रदशाकाले योगदो भवति ध्रुवम् ॥ ५ ॥

Stanza 5. – For one born in Virgo, Jupiter and Venus in the 4th produce Yoga in the course of their Dasas.

NOTES

Guru or Jupiter happens to be lord of the 4th while Venus is lord of the 9th. Thus the combination of the lords of the 4th and the 9th—a quadrant and a trine respectively, results in Rajayoga and the planets therefore are empowered to give good results in the course of their Dasas and Bhuktis. In actual practice it is found that Venus Dasa will be more beneficial than that of Jupiter, because Jupiter becomes afflicted, being lord of a Kendra.

कन्यायां जायमानस्य शनिलाभस्थितो यदि ।
शनेर्दाये च संप्राप्ते योगयुक्तो भवेन्नरः ॥ ६ ॥

Stanza 6.—A person born in Virgo Ascendant will enjoy beneficial results in the course of Saturn's Dasa provided Saturn is in the 11th.

अथ तुलालग्न विचारः ।
THULA LAGNA

तुलालग्ने तु जातस्य शनिर्योगप्रदो भवेत् ।
तृतीया षष्ठनाथोऽपि गुरुर्योगप्रदो भवेत् ॥ १ ॥

Stanza 1.—For one born in Libra, Saturn produces Yoga. Though lord of the 3rd and the 6th, Jupiter also becomes capable of producing Yoga.

NOTES

That Saturn becomes Yogakaraka for Libra Ascendant is understandable when we take into account that he owns the 4th and 5th houses. Jupiter is lord of the 3rd and the 6th and in this particular case he is supposed to produce Yoga for the simple reason that the 3rd and the 6th from Libra happen to be upachaya signs and hence beneficial. But the combination is quite against the ordinary rules of astrology which suggest that lords of the 3rd, the 6th and the 11th are always bad.

तुलालग्ने तु जातस्य धनसप्तमनायक: ।

न करोति कुज: पाप: निधनं तु न संशय: ॥ २ ॥

Stanza 2.—For a person born in Libra, Mars, though lord of the 2nd and the 7th and happens to be a malefic, does not kill the native. There is no doubt about it.

NOTES

Mars becomes a maraka and gets the death-inflicting power because he owns the 2nd and 7th houses. The author seems to opine that in spite of Mars becoming a maraka, he will not kill the native. Why he does not kill is not explained. Mars is a malefic planet and his owning a Kendra neutralises the evil. The power of neutralising can at best be interpreted as of some significance in the sense that Mars in the course of his Dasa may not cause much harm to the native. But this does not mean that he cannot kill the person In a number of horoscopes which we have in our possession there is ample evidence to show that Mars has killed thes native. Therefore in the light of actual experience one ha.'

to apply this stanza carefully so that the meaning may not be
literally interpreted.

तुलायां जायमानस्य गुरुशुक्रौ समन्वितौ ।

अन्योन्यं वीक्षितौ वापि भौममन्देन वीक्षितौ ॥ ३ ॥

Stanza 3.—For a person born in Libra if Jupiter
and Venus are together, or aspect each other, or get
themselves aspected by Saturn and Mars :

कुजभानुजस्थरूपौ गुरोःशुक्रांतरेपि वा ।

शुक्रादाये गुरोर्भुंक्ति कालेस्पोटव्रणादिकौ ॥ ४ ॥

Stanza 4.—Or they are in the signs owned by
Saturn and Mars, then during Jupiter Dasa, Venus
Bhukti or Venus Dasa, Jupiter Bhukti the native
suffers from smallpox, wounds or other similar
complaints.

NOTES

These two stanzas are important because they enable
the reader to predict what results pertaining to Jupiter are
produced during the sub-period of Venus, in the major
period of Jupiter or *vice versa* under certain given conditions.
They are :—(1) Jupiter and Venus should be in conjunction,
(2) or they should aspect each other, (3) or they both
should be aspected by Saturn and Mars, (4) or they should
be situated in the signs owned by Saturn and Mars.

If any of the above 4 combinations prevail, then the
person will suffer from smallpox, wounds and similar other
complaints. Here again much care is necessary on the part
of the astrologer to understand the exact significance
of the above combinations. In *Chart No 9,* Ascendant

is Libra ; Jupiter and Venus are in the 10th ; Saturn is in the Ascendant and Mars is in Capricorn. Thus almost all the conditions comprehended in the above two stanzas are satisfied. Jupiter and Venus are together in one side and both of them are aspected by Saturn and Mars. But yet the native did not suffer from smallpox but had only some wounds and cuts in the course of Jupiter Dasa. In such a typical horoscope a reader will notice that Jupiter is exalted, Mars is exalted and Saturn is exalted. Evidently the malefic influences which are supposed to accrue by a conglomeration of the evil effects are minimised for the simple reason that Jupiter's benefic effects have overpowered those of Mars.

	Chart No. 9 RASI 29-71		Jup. Venus
Mars			
		Ascdt. Sat.	

तुलायां जायमानस्य व्ययस्थौ भानुसोमजौ ।

शनिना वीक्षितौस्या तां मध्यायुर्भाग्यवान् पिता ॥ ५ ॥

Stanza 5.—For one born in Libra if the Sun and Mercury occupying the 12th are aspected by Saturn, the father will be fortunate and will live to middle age.

NOTES

Only one condition should be satisfied and that is both the Sun and Mercury should be in the 12th and they should be aspected by Saturn. The Sun is the Pitrukaraka and naturally his presence in the 12th aspected by Saturn is supposed to reduce the longevity of the father.

तुलालग्ने तु जातस्य रविस्सौरेरछुधस्य च ।

कुजस्य यदि संबन्धो बहुभाग्यप्रदो भवेत्   ॥ ६ ॥

Stanza 6.—For a person born in Libra if the Sun, Saturn and Mercury are in any way related to Mars either by combination or by aspect, then Mars becomes capable of producing immense good.

तुलालग्ने तु जातस्य रवेस्सौरेरबुधस्य च ।

कुजस्यवेंदुसंबधो राजयोग उदीरितः   ॥ ७ ॥

Stanza 7.—For one born in Libra if the Sun, Saturn and Mercury are combined with Mars or the Moon, Rajayoga is produced.

NOTES

The above two stanzas reveal that Mars is capable of doing much good if he is combined with the Sun, Saturn and Mercury and that Rajayoga is caused if the same three planets are combined with the Moon or Mars. Here again the respective places in which the combinations occur and the aspects good or bad to which the planets are subject seem to determine the nature and extent of Rajayoga.

तुलायां जायमानस्तु शुक्रसूर्यंबुधा यदि ।

लग्नस्थाः भाग्यवान् जातः धनवानश्च भवेध्रुवम्   ॥ ८ ॥

Stanza 8.—A person, born in Libra with the Sun, Venus and Mercury in the Ascendant, becomes fortunate and wealthy.

सौम्यमंदसितादित्याः लग्नस्थाश्चन्द्रभूमिजौ ।

सप्तमस्थो चन्द्रजस्य दशाकाले समागमे   ॥ ९ ॥

Stanza 9.—If Mercury, Saturn and Venus are in the Ascendant, or the Moon and Mars are in the 7th, then in the course of the Dasa of Mercury :

तुलायां जायमानास्तु पुरुषो धनवान् भवेत् ।

भाग्यवांश्चभवस्ये नवांशयो नास्थिवै ध्रुवम्   ॥ १० ॥

Stanza 10.—A person born in Libra Ascendant becomes rich and fortunate. There is no doubt about it.

NOTES

The above three stanzas indicate a combination under which one born in Libra can become rich and fortunate and the particular Dasa in which prosperity will be on the Ascendant. When the Sun, Venus and Mercury are in the Ascendant (Libra) then the Sun is debilitated, Venus is in his own house and Mercury lord of the 9th is in the Ascendant in a friendly house. The situation of Venus in the Ascendant (quadrant) cancels the effect of the debilitation of the Sun. Thus when the lord of the Ascendant (Venus), lord of the 9th (Mercury), lord of the 11th (the Sun) are together in the Ascendant, a powerful combination is produced. Added to these if Saturn is also in the Ascendant that will be an additional qualification because Saturn, a Yogakaraka for Libra Ascendant, exalted in the Ascendant fortifies the strength of the horoscope immensely. The good effects are further supplemented by the Moon and Mars being in the 7th causing what is called *Chandramangala Yoga* and hence the entire combination becomes unique in its own way.

अष्टमे तु गुरुर्भाग्ये मन्दोलाभे कुजेन्दुजौ ।

यदि सन्ति तृलाजातः राजयोग विशेषवान्   ॥ ११ ॥

Stanza 11.—For a person born in Libra a powerful Rajayoga is caused by the presence of Jupiter in the 8th, Saturn in the 9th and Mars and Mercury in the 11th.

षष्ठे वान्त्ये यदि गुरुर्लग्ने चन्द्रस्थितो भवेत् ।
शनेर्देदाये च संप्राप्ते घटजातो हि योगभाक् ॥ १२ ॥

Stanza 12.—A person born in Libra becomes fortunate during Saturn Dasa provided Jupiter is in the 6th or the 12th and the Moon is in the Ascendant.

तुलायां जायमानस्य मारको लग्नभार्गव: ।
द्वितीये सप्तमेशोऽपि न भौमो मारको भवेत् ॥ १३ ॥

Stanza 13.—For one born in Libra, Venus becomes a maraka if he is in the Ascendant. Mars does not become a maraka even though he is lord of the 2nd and the 7th.

NOTES

There was considerable controversy going on in the columns of THE ASTROLOGICAL MAGAZINE whether a planet which becomes the lord of the Ascendant can also become a maraka. This was a test question which several readers of THE ASTROLOGICAL MAGAZINE tried to answer in several ways. In Dr. Tagore's horoscope, according to Vimshottari, Jupiter lord of the Ascendant became the maraka. Another great writer held the view quoting from Parasara that lord of the Ascendant can never become a maraka. This was controverted by other well-known scholars who in spite of their contention that lord of the Ascendant under certain circumstances can become a maraka quoted in defence of their contention extracts from *Jataka Chandrika* and views propounded by Prof. B. Suryanarain Rao in his English Translation of *Jataka Chandrika*. In our humble opinion it is as clear as daylight that any planet can become a maraka irrespective of the fact, he is lord of the Ascendant or not. This view is supported by the above stanza when the author says that Venus becomes a maraka for people born in Libra Ascendant if he happens to stay in the Ascendant. And this is fully proved in a number of cases.

तुलायां जायमानस्य मन्दो लग्ने स्थितो यदि ।
कर्कटे यदि चन्द्रस्तु राजयोग उदीरितः ॥ १४ ॥

Stanza 14.—For one born in Libra, Rajayoga will be caused if Saturn is in the Ascendant and the Moon is in Cancer.

तुलाजातस्य मन्देज्य बुधभौमाः घटे यदि ।
राजस्थ राहुदाये तु पुण्यतीर्थफलम् भवेत् ॥ १५ ॥

Stanza 15.—A person born in Libra with Saturn, Jupiter, Mercury and Mars in Aquarius and Rahu in the 10th will undertake pilgrimages and have dips in sacred waters in the course of Rahu Dasa.

अथ वृश्चिकलग्न विचारः
VRISCHIKA LAGNA

वृश्चिके जायमानस्य गुरुसौम्य परस्परम् ।
संबन्धिनो यदि भवेद्द्विशेष धनयोगदै ॥ १ ॥

Stanza 1.—For a person born in Scorpio if Jupiter and Mercury are in conjunction or in mutual aspect, much wealth will be conferred.

तृतीयस्थौ यदि गुरुरौदार्यमधिकं भवेत् ।
सप्तमस्थास्सूर्यसौम्य शुक्रो यदि बुधस्य च ॥ २ ॥

Stanza 2.—If Jupiter is in the 3rd the native will have a charitable disposition.   If the Sun, Mercury and Venus are in the 7th :

दशाकाले तु संप्राप्ते वृश्चिकर्क्षे तु जातकः ।
राजयोगम् समाप्नोति महतीं कीर्तिमश्नुते ॥ ३ ॥

Stanza 3.—Then during the period (Dasa) of Mercury the person will enjoy much fame and power.

गुरुसौम्यौ पञ्चमस्थौ लाभे चन्द्रो भवेद्यदि ।
बहुभाग्य धनोपेतः कीटजन्मा न संशयः ॥ ४ ॥

Stanza 4.—A person born in Scorpio will undoubtedly become very fortunate and wealthy if Jupiter and Mercury are in the 5th and the Moon is in the 11th.

कीटजातस्य जीवेंधु केतुनो भाग्यगा यदि ।
गुरोर्दशा योगदाही केतोर्दायोव योगदः ॥ ५ ॥

Stanza 5.—For a person born in Scorpio if Jupiter, the Moon and Ketu are in the 9th house, fame and power will be conferred during Jupiter Dasa while Ketu Dasa will be ordinary.

NOTES

The author has devoted 22 stanzas for Pisces Ascendant while he has dispensed with Scorpio Ascendant within a short space. The combinations given are no doubt valuable. According to Parasara, Jupiter is a benefic for Scorpio Ascendant as he is lord of the 2nd and the 5th while a combination of the lords of the 9th and the 10th (the Moon and the Sun respectively) results in a Rajayoga. But in this work the author seems to stress on the importance of the mutual conjunction and aspect of Mercury and Jupiter. Mercury is evil as he is lord of the 8th and the 11th but he seems to lose the evil nature by being placed in the 7th house with Venus and the Sun (*vide* stanza 2 *supra*) to the extent that during his Dasa, Mercury will confer fame and power. The temporary evil of ownership, acquired by Mercury, seems to disappear by his presence in Pisces with Jupiter and by the Moon being in Virgo or the 11th. This combination (stanza 4) may be diagrammatically represented thus as in Chart No. 10 below.

Jupiter Merc.			
	Chart No. 10		
	Ascdt.		Moon

Stanza 4 gives the combination for immense wealth and fortune. Jupiter is the lord of wealth and fortune and he is in the 5th aspected by the Moon lord of the 9th. There is thus Gajakesari Yoga also which will further fortify the house of wealth. Mercury though evil (by lordship) happens to be lord of gains and the forces of the 2nd, the 5th, the 9th and the 11th focussed on the 5th house give rise to a distinct Dhana Yoga. The principle adumbrated in stanza 5 may be further extended thus :

(1) The Moon may be in Pisces and Jupiter and Mercury in Virgo.

(2) The Moon may be in Pisces, Jupiter in Cancer and Mercury in Virgo.

(3) The Moon and Mercury may be in Pisces and Jupiter in Cancer.

(4) The Moon and Mercury may be in Pisces and Jupiter in Virgo.

(5) Mercury may be in Virgo, the Moon in Pisces and Jupiter in Cancer.

(6) Mercury may be in Cancer, the Moon in Virgo and Jupiter in Pisces.

Other permutations and combinations may also be obtained similarly.

Stanza 9 comprehends the presence of a very powerful Gajakesari Yoga while the presence of Ketu with the Moon and Jupiter seems to deprive Ketu of the power of conferring any Yoga during his own Dasa.

अथ धनुर्लग्न विचार:

DHANUR LAGNA

धनुर्लग्ने तु जातस्य पञ्चमस्थ शनेर्देशा ।

शुभप्रदायोगदेति वदंति विभुदोत्तमाः ॥ १ ॥

Stanza 1.—For a person born in Sagittarius Saturn produces good results and confers Yoga in his Dasa, if he is in the 5th house.

धनुलॆग्ने तु जातस्य लाभस्थो योगदश्शनिः ।
इतरक्षे तु जातस्य लाभमन्दो न योगदः ॥ २ ॥

Stanza 2.—For a person born in Sagittarius Saturn in the 11th confers Yoga ; for a person born in other Ascendants Saturn in the 11th does not cause any Yoga.

धनुजंस्य भृगु रवि भाग्ये मन्दस्तृतीयगः ।
शनिदाँग्ये तु भवतो भाग्ययोग धनागमौ ॥ ३ ॥

Stanza 3.—A person born in Sagittarius, with the Sun and Venus in the 9th and Saturn in the 3rd, will enjoy fame and wealth in the course of Saturn Dasa.

कुम्मे भौम रवि राहु सिंहगो यदि तद्दृशा ।
कालेद्युसरितस्नम् धनुजॊतस्समश्नुते ॥ ४ ॥

Stanza 4.—A person born in Sagittarius, with Mars and the Sun in Aquarius and Rahu in Leo, will have a bath in the sea in Rahu Dasa.

NOTES

A careful reading into the above stanzas seems to bring out one important fact. *viz.*, the lord of the 11th (who is generally declared evil) produces good results if he is in conjunction with a trinal lord or quadrangular lord (who is a natural malefic). For example on page 48 stanza I while dealing with Scorpio Ascendant, the author seems to imply that Dhana Yoga is caused by the conjunction or mutual aspect of Jupiter and Mercury. Jupiter is no doubt a natural benefic. But for Scorpio Ascendant, he becomes a trinal

lord (trikonadhipati) while Mercury is lord of the 8th and
the 11th. Again in stanza 2 under Scorpio Ascendant,
Mercury Dasa is said to confer Rajayoga, if Mercury is in
the 7th with Venus and the Sun. Venus as *Kendradhipati*
becomes evil while the Sun alone is a (temporary) benefic
as owning the 10th.

Again in stanza 3 under Sagittarius Ascendant the
author makes it clear that Saturn produces good in his Dasa
if he is in Aquarius and the Sun and Venus are in the 9th
or Leo. Venus is lord of the 11th for Sagittarius and his
association with the Sun means—association with a trinal
lord. Unless Venus loses (some of) the evil effects of his
11th house lordship, his aspect over Saturn cannot be
construed as so good as to enable Saturn to confer wealth
and fame in his Dasa. Saturn and the Sun are bitter enemies ;
the Sun and Venus are bitter enemies. Only Saturn and
Venus are friends. The conjunction of the Sun (9th lord)
and Venus (11th lord) in the 9th—like poles being brought
together—seems to repel each other's bad qualities and
rendering the aspect of Venus favourable. I may not be quite
correct in my explanations. But this is how I understand the
principle and I am open to conviction. The author gives
peculiar combinations and as far as my humble experience
goes most of them seem to satisfy practical application.

अथ मकरलग्न विचार:

MAKARA LAGNA

मकरे जायमानस्य अष्टमस्थो भवेद्बुध: ।
लग्नसंस्थो यदि गुरु शुक्रेण च निरीक्षित: ॥ १ ॥

Stanza 1. -- For a person born in Capricorn if Mercury is in the 8th and Jupiter is in the Ascendant aspected by Venus,

दीर्घायुर्योगमाप्नोति जातस्तत्र न संशयः ।

निर्धनश्च भवेज्जातोह्यत्रापि च न संशयः ॥ २ ॥

Stanza 2. —Long life will no doubt be conferred, but poverty will also be undoubtedly caused.

मकरे जायमानस्य पञ्चमस्थेद् भृगुरुशुभः ।

राज्यस्थश्चेद्भृगुर्योगं न ददाति कदाचन ॥ ३ ॥

Stanza 3. —For a person born in Capricorn Venus in the 5th house is good; if however he is in the 10th, he may not give rise to any Yoga.

मकरे जायमानस्य लग्नस्थौ शुक्रचन्द्रजौ ।

पञ्चमस्थश्च चन्द्रस्तु गुरुणा वीक्षितो यदि ॥ ४ ॥

Stanza 4. —One born in Capricorn with Venus and Mercury in the Ascendant and the Moon in the 5th aspected by Jupiter.

मण्डलाधीश्वरो राज भवदेत्र न संशयः ।

भृहज्जातकयोगोऽयं महाराजक संज्ञिकः ॥ ५ ॥

Stanza 5. —Will undoubtedly become an emperor. This Yoga is termed as **Maharaja Yoga** according to *Brihat Jataka*.

लग्नसंस्थो यदि गुरुर्लासे शुक्र कुजो यदि ।

गुरुदाये तु संप्राप्ते आतृ मूल धनागमः ॥ ६ ॥

Stanza 6.—If Jupiter is in the Ascendant and Venus and Mars are in the 11th, the native will get money through brothers in the course of Jupiter Dasa.

अंधोल्लिका वाहनां च मकरे जातको नरः ।
लभते नात्र संदेहस्सूरिभिः परिकीर्तितः ॥ ७ ॥

Stanza 7.—The learned in astrology have said that a person born in Capricorn will get access to palanquins and other conveyances.

रविचंद्र बुधालग्ने व्ययो शुक्र कुजा यदि ।
भ्रातृभाग्यम् स्वभाग्यं च प्राप्नोति मृगजो नरः ॥ ८ ॥

Stanza 8.—If the Sun, the Moon and Mercury are in the Ascendant and Mars and Venus are in the 12th, the native will not only get wealth from brothers but will also earn himself.

मृगजन्मा मन्दसौम्य भाग्यस्थो भाग्यवान् भवेत् ।
व्ययस्थो राहु जीवौ तु राहुर्योगप्रदो भवेत् ॥ ९ ॥

Stanza 9.—For a person born in Capricorn, Saturn and Mercury in the 9th confer fortune. Rahu becomes Yogakaraka if he is in the 12th with Jupiter.

मकरे जायमानस्य चन्द्रः कर्कटके स्थितः ।
मकरस्थ धरासूनु राजयोगप्रदो भवेत् ॥ १० ॥

Stanza 10.—For a person born in Capricorn, Rajayoga is caused by the presence of the Moon in Cancer and Mars in Capricorn.

NOTES

The stanzas are clear enough and need no further explanations. However, some of the statements are vague and leave the reader where he is without making him understand the principles clearly. The 1st and 2nd stanzas suggest that Mercury no doubt bestows longevity if he is in the 8th but the native will suffer from poverty. This is quite consistent. Because Mercury is lord of the 9th or fortune, he will be occupying the 12th or house of loss (from the 9th) if he is in the 8th from the Ascendant, thus causing loss of fortune.

Venus is the Yogakaraka for Capricorn. Whilst he will produce good results in the 5th, his presence in the 10th is not approved. For Capricorn Venus not only owns a trine (Taurus) but also a quadrant. When he is in the 5th it is good because as lord of a trine he will be in a trine. He also owns a quadrant (Libra) and this is bad for a benefic. Coupled with this, if he also occupies a quadrant, he will be powerless to produce any Rajayoga. Quadrangular ownership (Kendradhipatya for benefics and that too for Jupiter and Venus) is held to be productive of extremely bad results. Stanza 6 hints at a distinct Neechabhanga Rajayoga with particular reference to Capricorn. If Jupiter is in the Ascendant he is Neecha. But if Venus a Yogakaraka for Capricorn is in the 11th with Mars (the planet who gets exalted in Capricorn) the debilitation effect is cancelled with the result that Jupiter gives money through brothers (because Mars, responsible for cancellation of Neecha, is karaka of brothers and Jupiter is lord of the house of brothers). Stanza 7 is vague because every one born in Capricorn Ascendant cannot aspire to possess palanquins and conveyances.

The Rajayoga implied in stanga 9 by the conjunction of Saturn (lord of the Ascendant) and Mercury (lord of the 9th) in the 9th is understandable even according to ordinary canons of astrology.

अथ कुम्भलग्न विचार:

KUMBHA LAGNA

कुम्मे सिंहे तु जातस्य योगो नैव विशेषक: ।
भाग्यराज्येश सम्बन्धमावेणेति विदुरभुधा: ॥ १ ॥

Stanza 1.—The learned in astrology have said that for persons born in Aquarius and Leo Ascendants no particular Yoga is caused by the mere combination of the lords of the 9th and the 10th.

लग्ने शु॰ वराज्ये राहुर्वा कुम्भसद्मन: ।
गुरुराहुदशाकाले योगदो भवतो ध्रुवम् ॥ २ ॥

Stanza 2.—For a person born in Aquarius, if Venus is in the Ascendant, the Sun is in the 10th and Rahu is in Aquarius, Yoga will be caused in the Dasas of Rahu and Jupiter.

कुम्मे तु जायमानस्य रन्ध्रस्थौ रविभूमिजौ ।
तयोर्दाये दु:खदस्या बुधदाये हि योगद: ॥ ३ ॥

Stanza 3.—For a person born in Aquarius if the Sun and Mars are in the 8th, sorrow will be caused in their Dasas. But during Mercury Dasa good will result.

घटजाबस्य लग्नस्थो गृरुमंदो द्वितीयगः ।

गुरुदाये मिश्रयोगः शनिदायेव योगदः ॥ ४ ॥

Stanza 4.—For a person born in Aquarius, if Jupiter is in the Ascendant and Saturn is in the 2nd, mixed results will be produced in Jupiter Dasa and no good will be produced in Saturn Dasa.

कुम्मे तु जायमानस्य शनि शुक्रौ तु लाभगौ ।

शुक्रदाये च संप्राप्ते शुक्रो भवति योगदः ॥ ५ ॥

Stanza 5.—Venus gives rise to Yoga in his Dasa if Saturn and Venus are in the 11th house.

विक्रमस्थास्सूर्यसौम्या जीवश्चेत्सूर्यंदायके ।

रविश्शुभप्रदस्सत्यम् कुम्भजातस्य राज्यदः ॥ ६ ॥

Stanza 6.—For a person born in Aquarius if the Sun, Mercury and Jupiter are in the 3rd, the Sun becomes beneficial and capable of conferring political power.

NOTES

The author has stressed on the negative value of the association of lords of the 9th and the 10th in producing Rajayoga, *e.g.*, Mars' ownership of the 10th, devoid of corresponding ownership of a trinal house. We have to humbly differ from the author's view because the combination of the lords of the 9th and the 10th has been found to produce quite auspicious results in actual practice. Moreover, the author of *Jataka Chandrika* inclines to the view that combination of Venus and Mars produces Raja Yoga (vide *Jataka Chandrika*, English translation by Prof. B. Suryanarain Rao).

Parasara has clearly stated in his *Brihat Parasara Hora* that Venus alone is a benefic for Aquarius Ascendant—*Daitya Guruh Shubhah*—and he further says that Mars produces Rajayoga. We do not know what prompted the author of this book to observe that mere combination of the lords of the 9th and the 10th does not produce any good. Probably he implies that the combination, to be productive of good, should occur in certain beneficial houses.

The Parivarthana Yoga implied in stanza 4 about Jupiter being in the Ascendant and Saturn being in the 2nd, deserves our careful attention. Instead of Saturn being in the 2nd if he

Chart No. 11.—*Born on 27/28-5-1903 at 1-19 a.m. Lat. 9° N. ; Long. 77° 42' E.*

	RASI					NAVAMSA		
Ketu	Sun Moon Mercury (R)	Venus	Mars			Sun Venus	Saturn Ascdt. Jupiter
Ascdt. Jupiter							Rahu
Saturn (R)			Ketu				Moon Mercury
		Mars Rahu					

Balance of Mercury's Dasa at birth : years 5-4-24.

aspects the 2nd house—and Jupiter is in the Ascendant, even Saturn Dasa will produce quite beneficial results. If however the 2nd house is aspected by Jupiter and the Ascendant is aspected by Saturn, both the Dasas of Jupiter and of Saturn will produce beneficial results building up the career of the native.

In *Chart No. 11*, Jupiter is in the Ascendant while Saturn Lagnadhipati, instead of being placed in Pisces, aspects Pisces from his own sign Capricorn. The dignity of a planet in any given combination should always be judged after a careful consideration of its disposition both in the Rasi and Navamsa. From the Moon, Saturn owns the 9th and 10th houses and aspects the 2nd house. Hence the Dasa of Saturn will be conducive for financial prosperity.

In *Chart No. 12*, Jupiter aspects the 2nd, Saturn aspects the Ascendant – each Bhava being aspected by its own lord. This combination is quite conducive for the financial prosperity of the native during both the Dasas of Jupiter and Saturn.

Chart No. 12.—*Born on 8-8-1912 at about 7–23 p.m. L.M.T. Lat. 13° N. ; Long. 5h. 10m. 20s. E*

Rahu		Moon Saturn			Saturn	Venus	
Ascdt.	RASI		Sun	Rahu Sun	NAVAMSA		Ketu Moon Mercury
			Mars Merc. Venus	Ascdt.			
	Jupiter		Ketu		Jupiter	Mars	

Balance of Mars' Dasa at birth : years 6-0-10.

अथ मीनलग्न विचारः

MEENA LAGNA

मीने कुम्मे च जातस्य व्ययशुक्रो न योगदः ।

इतरे जायमानस्य व्ययशुक्रुभप्रदः:   ॥ १ ॥

Stanza 1.—For a person born in Pisces or
Aquarius, Venus in the 12th does not give rise to any
Yoga. For a person born in other Ascendants Venus
in the 12th produces benefic results.

मीनलग्ने तु जातस्य व्ययमन्दो हि योगदः ।

लग्रात् व्यये स्थितश्चन्द्रो धनहीनो भवेन्नरः   ॥ २ ॥

Stanza 2.—For a person born in Pisces Ascendant, Saturn in the 12th is good. The native
becomes bereft of wealth if the Moon is in the 12th.

मीनलग्ने तु जातस्य गुरोर्दांये समागमे ।

चद्रांतभुंक्तिकालस्तु पूर्वैयोगस्वहृसदः ॥ ३ ॥

Stanza 3.—For a person born in Pisces, the
Yoga referred to earlier becomes reduced in the sub-
period of the Moon, in the Dasa of Jupiter.

NOTES

The only Yoga referred to above is the presence of Saturn
in the 12th. Stanza 3 reads that the Yoga becomes ineffective
or reduced in Jupiter Dasa, Moon's Bhukti. In other words
for a person born in Pisces, Saturn's situation in the 12th or
Aquarius results in a Yoga and the indications of this Yoga
get reduced in the course of Jupiter Dasa, Moon's Bhukti.
Stanza 3 is not at all clear because it has not explained how

the Yoga generated as per stanza 2 could get obstructed in
the Dasa of Jupiter within the Bhukti of the Moon.

Chart No. 13.—*Born on 24-3-1883 at 6 a.m. (L M.T.)*
Lat. 13° N. ; Long. 77° 35' E.

Sun Ascdt.	Ketu	Saturn	Jupit.	Mars	Mercury Rahu	Moon	
Mars Mercury		RASI				NAVAMSA	
Venus	HJH–39			Sat.			
		Rahu	Moon			Ascdt. Sun Jupiter Ketu	Venus

Balance of Moon's Dasa at birth : years 5-11-16.

In the above horoscope (Chart No. 13) Saturn aspects
the 12th. Let us assume that some Yoga is caused. In
Jupiter Dasa Moon's Bhukti, the native lost his eye sight
and became completely dependent upon others. What
connection these particular directions had with Saturn and the
loss of eye sight, intelligent readers must anticipate. Stanzas
2 and 3 may be interpreted to mean that if Saturn is in the
12th house or aspects the 12th, then during the Moon's sub-
period in the Dasa of Jupiter, the person will suffer from
sorrows, troubles, loss of organs and other misfortunes.

मीनलग्ने तु जातस्य पञ्चमस्थो गुरुर्यदि ।
स्त्रीसन्तति समृद्धिस्यात् कुत्रचित्पुत्र सन्ततिः ॥ ४ ॥

Stanza 4.—A person born in Pisces with Jupiter in the 5th will have more daughters and few sons.

मीनलग्ने तु जातस्य द्वितीये यदि चन्द्रमाः ।
पञ्चमस्थो यदि कुजश्चन्द्रदाये धनागमः ॥ ५ ॥

Stanza 5.—The person will have access to wealth in Moon's Dasa if the Moon is in the 2nd, and Mars is in the 5th.

मीने तु जायमानस्य गुरुषष्ठेऽष्टमे भृगुः ।
भाग्ये शनिश्चन्द्रकुजौ लाभेचोत्कृष्टभाग्यवान् ॥ ६ ॥

Stanza 6.—The person will become highly fortunate if Jupiter is in the 6th, Venus is in the 8th, Saturn is in the 9th, and Mars and the Moon are in the 11th.

मीने तु जायमानस्य चन्द्रसौम्यकुजा यदि ।
मकरस्था यदि भवन् धन वाहन योगदाः ॥ ७ ॥

Stanza 7.—A person born in Pisces will possess wealth and vehicles if the Moon, Mercury and Mars are in Capricorn.

मीने जातस्य लग्नस्थो शनिचन्द्रौ च लाभगः ।
कुजष्ठेकविशुक्रदाये भाग्यमुदीरितम् ॥ ८ ॥

Stanza 8.—Predict fortune in Venus Dasa for one born in Pisces Ascendant, if Saturn and the Moon are in the Ascendant, Mars is in the 11th and Venus is in the 6th.

मीने तु जायमानस्य सोम्यजीवेन्दु भूमिजाः ।
चतुर्थस्था यदि भवन् शुक्रेण रहिता यदि ॥ ९ ॥

Stanza 9.—For a person born in Pisces, if Mercury, Jupiter, the Moon and Mars except Venus are in the 4th house—

तद्दशान्तर्दशाकाले कीर्तिमाप्नोति शाश्वतम् ।
र्सिंहासनस्थो भवति राजराजो भवेन्नरः ॥ १० ॥

Stanza 10.—Then in the course of the Dasas of these planets (except Venus) he will be crowned as a King and will enjoy much fame.

मीनजातस्य पुंसस्तु लग्नराज्याधिपो गुरुः ।
राज्ये स्थितो यदि भवेद्योगदश्च भवे ध्रुवम् ॥ ११ ॥

Stanza 11.—For a person in Pisces Rajayoga is certainly caused if the lord of the Ascendant and the 10th, *viz.*, Jupiter occupies the 10th.

मीनजातस्य वृषभे चेन्दुस्सिंहे रविर्यदि ।
कन्यायां सोमपुत्रस्तु घटे शुक्रो धनुर्गुरुः ॥ १२ ॥

Stanza 12.—For a person born in Pisces the Moon in Taurus, the Sun in Leo, Mercury in Virgo, Venus in Libra and Jupiter in Sagittarius.

कुम्भे शनिः कुजोल्लग्ने बहुभाग्यमुदीरितम् ।
एकद्विखचराभ्यां वा हीनोपूर्वर्क्षं संगमः ॥ १३ ॥

Stanza 13.—Saturn in Aquarius and Mars in the 11th give rise to much fortune. If one or two combinations as per previous stanza are not present,

भाग्यवान् गुणवान्श्चैव महतीं कीर्तिमश्नुते ।
बृहज्जातकयोगोयम् विद्वद्भिः परिकीर्तितः ॥ १४ ॥

Stanza 14.—The person becomes not only fortunate and of good character but will also get immense fame. This Yoga is Brihatjataka Yoga.

NOTES

All the stanzas are clear excepting the last three which mean that for a person born in Pisces, a great Yoga will be caused by the presence of the Sun, Mercury, Venus, Jupiter and Saturn in their own houses, and the Moon and Mars in their exaltation houses. Stanza 13 says that if out of the above, one or two dispositions—the Sun in Leo and the Moon in Taurus or Mars in Capricorn and Mercury in Virgo and so on—are not present, even then the full effects of the Yoga will be conferred.

Thus ends the First Chapter entitled Lagna Yoga in BHAVARTHA RATNAKARA of Sri Ramanujacharya.

CHAPTER II

अथ धनयोग विचारः

DHANA YOGAS

धनेश पञ्चमस्थे च पञ्चमेशो धने यदि ।
धनपे लाभगे वापि लाभेशो धनगो यदि ॥ १ ॥

Stanza 1.—If the lord of the 2nd is in the 5th and the lord of the 5th is in the 2nd or if the lord of the 2nd is in the 11th and the lord of the 11th is in the 2nd,

पञ्चमेशो पञ्चमे वा भाग्ये भाग्याधिपो यदि ।
विशेष धनयोगाश्चेत्याहुर्जातककोविदाः ॥ २ ॥

Stanza 2.—If the lord of the 5th is in the 5th and the lord of the 9th is in the 9th, the learned in astrology say that much wealth will be earned.

धनलाभाधिपत्योर्हि धनयोगमू नवै विना ।
नवपञ्चमेशयोरन्यरेण सहसंगति ॥ ३ ॥

Stanza 3.—Dhana Yoga will result if the lords of the 2nd and 11th are combined with lords of the 5th and 9th. If such 2nd and 11th lords are conjoined by

other lords (than 5th and 9th) no Dhana Yoga will be
formed.

विशेष धनयोगस्य चाभावे व्यस्तिस्खलपकम् ।

इति दैवज्ञमणयो वदंति विसुदोत्तमाः ॥ ४ ॥

Stanza 4.—Though immense wealth may not
result, the native will earn some wealth. Thus opine
the learned in astrology.

Chart No. 14.—*Born on 23-10-1898 at 11-30 p.m.
(L.M.T.) ; Lat. 19° 10' N. ; Long. 75° E.*

		Ketu		Ketu	
		Mars Ascdt.			
	RASI			NAVAMSA	
Moon			Venus Merc.		Mars
Rahu	Venus Saturn	Sun Mercury Jupiter	Sun Sat.	Jupiter Rahu	Ascdt. Moon

Balance of Mars' Dasa at birth :   years 4-9-29.

NOTES

Stanzas 1 to 3 are clear enough. Stanza 4 means that if
the lords of the 2nd and the 11th are combined with other
lords than those of the 5th and the 9th, the Dhana Yoga
referred to in stanza 3 will not manifest itself in full but there
will be access to wealth on a humble scale. The majority
of horoscopes belong to this category.

In *Chart No. 14* lord of the 2nd the Sun is aspected by Mars lord of the 5th. Lord of the 2nd is also in conjunction with the lord of the 9th, Jupiter. These have given rise to much wealth.

धनलाभाधिपत्योश्च व्ययेशेन सहस्थितिः ।
संबन्धो यदि विद्येत धनाधिक्यं न विद्यते   ॥ ५ ॥

Stanza 5.—Much wealth will not be acquired if the lords of the 2nd and the 11th are combined with the lord of the 12th.

Chart No. 15.—*Born on 14-5-1896 at 17-0 Gh. at Lat. 13° N. ; Long. 77° 35' E.*

Mars	Venus	Sun Moon Mercury		Saturn	Ascdt. Ketu
Rahu			Jupit		Moon
	RASI		Ketu Ascdt.	NAVAMSA	Mars Mercury
	III-61		Sun		
		Saturn	Rahu	Jupiter	Venus

Balance of Moon's Dasa at birth : years 2-5-21.

NOTES

In *Chart No. 15* Mercury lord of the 2nd and the 11th is with the Moon lord of the 12th. The native possesses ordinary wealth. There are several afflictions in this horoscope especially, the Dwirdwadasa positions of planets.

गुरोश्च धनकारस्य धनाधिपतिना सहा ।
संबन्धश्च बुधेनापि धनयोग उदीरितः ॥ ६ ॥

Stanza 6.—Dhana Yoga is found if Jupiter is conjoined with the lord of the 2nd and Mercury.

लाभेशो लाभगोवाऽपि लग्नेशो लग्नेशो यदि ।
धनेशो धनगश्चैव धनयोग इतीरितः ॥ ७ ॥

Stanza 7.—Dhana Yoga is also caused if lords of the 11th, the 1st and the 2nd are in their respective houses.

धनेशो लाभाराशिशः उभौ लग्नगतौ यदि ।
धनयोग इति प्रोक्तः बुधैर्जातककोविदैः ॥ ८ ॥

Stanza 8.—Learned astrologers say that Dhana Yoga would result if both the lords of the 2nd and the 11th are in the Ascendant.

NOTES

Three more combinations are given in stanzas 6, 7 and 8 for the acquisition of money, *viz.*, (*a*) the 11th, 2nd and 1st lords should be in their respective houses, (*b*) Jupiter must be combined with lord of the 2nd and Mercury and (*c*) lords of the 2nd and the 11th should be in the Ascendant. Combinations are simple enough to understand. In this horoscope *(Chart No. 16)* Jupiter himself is lord of the 2nd and he is in a kendra. Jupiter is also lord of the 11th. These two combinations are indicative of much wealth especially in Jupiter Dasa.

Chart No. 16.—*Born on 8-8-1912 at about 7-23 p.m. (L.M.T.) at Lat. 13° N. ; Long. 77° 35' E.*

Rahu		Saturn Moon		Saturn	Venus
Ascdt.	RASI		Sun	Sun Rahu	NAVAMSA
			Mars Merc. Venus	Ascdt.	Ketu Moon Mercury
	Jupiter		Ketu	Jupiter	Mars

Balance of Mars' Dasa at birth : years 6—0—10.

Chart No. 17.—*Born on 28/29-8-1898 at 5-33 a.m. (L.M.T.) at Lat. 61° 50' N. ; Long. 5h. 3m. E.*

		Mars Ketu		Moon	Ketu	Jupiter
	RASI			NAVAMSA		Ascdt.
Moon	3-7		Sun Ascdt. Merc.			Sun
Rahu	Saturn		Jupit. Venus	Merc.	Mars Saturn Rahu	Venus

Balance of Moon's Dasa at birth : years 9—8—12.

In this horoscope *(Chart No. 17)* lord of the 2nd and the 11th is Mercury and he is in the Ascendant, a very good combination for wealth. The native has earned considerably and is well off financially

सर्वेषु भवस्थानेषु तत्तद्भावादिकारकः ।
विद्यते तस्यभावस्य फलम् खल्पमुदीरितम्   ॥ ९ ॥

Stanza 9.—If the different Karakas are present in their respective Bhavas, such Bhavas lose vitality and give rise to very little of their indications.

NOTES

This is an important stanza. It says that Bhavas will be destroyed if they are occupied by their respective Karakas. The Sun is *Pitrukaraka* the indicator of father ; the Moon indicator of mother *(Matrukaraka)* ; Mars—brothers ; Mercury— karma or profession ; Jupiter—children ; Venus—wife ; Saturn—longevity ; Rahu–maternal relations ; and Ketu paternal relations. The 9th house rules father and the Sun is the Karaka of father. If the Sun is in the 9th, then the 9th Bhava becomes afflicted. Mars in the 3rd affects the brothers and so on. Saturn seems to be an exception as also Jupiter. If Saturn—the Karaka of longevity—is in the 8th, house of longevity, then instead of reducing the longevity Saturn confers long life. Similarly if Jupiter, Karaka for wealth, is in the 2nd, then the 2nd house indications are promoted. These are exceptions to the general rule.

सप्तमाधिपतिश्चन्द्रो धनस्थाने स्थितो यदि ।
केवलेन्दुश्च धनगो नष्टद्रव्यागमो भवेत्   ॥ १० ॥

Stanza   10.—If the Moon happening to be the
lord of the 7th is in the 2nd, alone, the native gets
back his lost wealth.

NOTES

This is possible only in case of Capricorn horoscopes.
Here the author emphasises that the very presence of the
Moon in the 2nd secures for the native, lost wealth if any.
When the 7th lord is in the 2nd it is clear that the person gets
money through the 7th house indications such as marriage
and business partners.

Chart No. 18.—*Born   on   16–10–1981   at   2-26 p.m.
(I.S.T.) at Lat. 13° N. ; Long. 77° 35' E.*

	Ketu	Jupit.		Saturn Jupiter	
Moon	RASI		Rahu	NAVAMSA	Venus
Ascdt.		Sat.	Moon		Ketu
Mars Rahu	Mercury Sun	Venus	Mars	Mercury Sun	Ascdt.

Balance of Rahu's Dasa at birth : years 11–8–20.

In *Chart No. 18* the Moon lord of the 7th is in the 2nd.
The native has not lost any wealth. But after the marriage

the financial circumstances have improved considerably. Note also the presence of Saturn, Ayushkaraka in the 8th or Ayusthana suggesting long life. The author has not referred to modifications of results in the above combinations if the Moon is aspected and otherwise conjoined. However, it is understood that aspectal and conjunctional peculiarities have a modifying or qualifying influence

अथ निर्धनयोग विचारः

COMBINATIONS FOR POVERTY

लग्नवाहन भाग्येशाझ्झष्टमस्थान संस्थिताः ।
जातो जननमारभ्य महद्दारिद्रमइनुते ॥ १ ॥

Stanza 1.—If the lords of the Ascendant, the 4th and the 9th are in the 8th, the person suffers poverty from his very birth.

धनेशे व्ययभावस्थे व्ययेशो धनगो यदि ।
जातस्य निर्धनो योगो वक्तव्यस्य सदा बुधैः ॥ २ ॥

Stanza 2.—If the lord of the 2nd is in the 12th and the lord of the 12th is in the 2nd, the native always suffers from poverty.

धनेशो व्ययराशौस्यात् व्ययेशे लग्नगे यदि ।
मारकग्रहसंदृष्टौ निर्धनश्च भवेन्नरः ॥ ३ ॥

Stanza   3.—A person becomes bereft of wealth if the lord of the 2nd is in the 12th and the lord of the 12th is in the Ascendant aspected by a maraka planet.

पञ्चमेशो रिपुस्थश्चेद्राग्येशो रन्ध्रगो यदि ।
मारकग्रह संदृष्टौ निर्धनश्च भवेन्नरः ॥ ४ ॥

Stanza   4.—Poverty is indicated if the lord of the 5th is in the 6th, and the lord of the 9th is in the 8th aspected by a maraka planet.

NOTES

The author now gives four combinations for poverty. A careful consideration of these combinations suggests that poverty will result by certain malefic dispositions of the lords of the Ascendant, the 2nd, the 5th and the 9th. Whatever may be the nature of combinations causing poverty or wealth, the strong and powerful disposition of Ascendant and its lord will exercise a powerful influence in maintaining the *status quo* of the native in the different spheres of his activities. The combinations for poverty mentioned in the above stanzas are :

1. Lords of the Ascendant, the 4th and the 9th, should be in the 8th. If all the above three lords are in the 8th, the native will be very poor. By implication it means that if one or two of the above lords are in the 8th, the degree of poverty is lessened. There is a lot of difference between a person who is very poor and starving and one who is moderately poor and can afford at least some of the necessities of life. Prof. B. Suryanarain Rao has dealt with these combinations in a masterly way in his book *Sarwartha Chintamani* and the reader will do well to refer to the English Translation of this famous book.

2. There must be parivarthana or exchange of places between the 2nd and 12th lords. If the 2nd lord is in the 12th and the 12th lord is in the 2nd, extreme poverty will result. If the 2nd lord is in the 12th but the latter is not in the 2nd, and if the 12th lord is in the 2nd but the latter is not in the 12th, the degree of poverty will vary. These niceties should be carefully noted in making predictions as otherwise one is bound to hit off the mark in his conclusions.

3. The third combination suggests that poverty is caused by the lord of wealth being in the 12th and the 12th lord being in the Ascendant aspected by a maraka.

This means that if the maraka does not aspect the lord of the 12th in the 1st, then poverty should not be predicted.

4. The lord of the 5th in the 6th and the lord of the 9th in the 8th aspected by a maraka will also result in poverty. If the combination is devoid of the aspect of a maraka though much poverty may not result, the native will have to struggle and he will not have a smooth financial career. Poverty is held to be the greatest curse by most of the people while the greatest sages have scorned wealth, as the greatest obstacle in the way of spiritual realisation.

I am herewith giving two typical horoscopes. In Chart No. 19 lord of the 9th is in the 8th while lord of the 2nd is in the 12th. These two combinations have not made the person utterly poor because the 6th is not occupied by the lord of the 5th and the lord of the 12th is not in the 9th, while lord of the 4th is in the 4th; lord of the Ascendant is in the 9th. Thus even though two combinations for poverty are present, the favourable disposition of lords of the Ascendant and the 4th have acted as an antidote for poverty. The native is a middle class man.

Chart No. 19.—*Born on 10-5-1903 at Gh. 27-30 after sunrise. Lat. 13° N. ; Long. 77° 35' E.*

Ketu	Sun	Mercury	Venus			Jupiter	Mercury Saturn
Jupiter	RASI			Moon Mars	NAVAMSA		Rahu
Saturn	III–51			Ketu			
		Ascdt. Moon	Rahu Mars		Ascdt. Venus Sun		

Balance of Rahu Dasa at birth : years 6–7–19.

In Chart No.—20 lord of the 4th and the 9th, Mars, is in the 8th. Mars is a Yogakaraka for Leo Ascendant and his situation in the 8th has taken away the value of the horoscope. The native belongs to a respectable family but is immersed in debts. Readers must be able to differentiate between different kinds of poverty. One is born poor and continues to be so throughout life, while the other born in the lap of luxury suffers from the pangs of poverty by his extravagant habits, and is always bothered by creditors. I am giving the horoscope of a person who occupied a very good position as an Engineer but died grovelling in debts. He was worried by his creditors even on his death-bed. The combinations in the following chart (No. 21) should be carefully noted and marked. Lord of the Ascendant, Mercury, is in the 8th ; lord of the 2nd, the Moon, is in the 12th with

Chart No. 20.—*Born on 15-4-1883 at 1-30 p.m.*
Lat. 30° N. ; Long. 76° E.

Mars	Sun Mercury Ketu	Saturn	Jupit.			Rahu Mercury Ascdt.	Sun Venus	
Venus			Moon	Sat.				
	RASI III-59		Ascdt.			NAVAMSA		Mars
		Rahu				Moon Jupiter	Ketu	

Balance of Saturn's Dasa at birth : years 1–5–3.

Chart No. 21.—*Born on 17-2-1891 at 2 p.m. (L.M.T.)*
Lat. 13° N. ; Long. 77° 35′ E.

Mars		Moon Rahu	Ascdt.				Mercury	Rahu
Sun Jupiter					Mars			
	RASI					NAVAMSA		Moon
Mercury	III-61		Sat.		Ascdt.			
Venus	Ketu				Sun Ketu	Jupiter Saturn	Venus	

Balance of Mars' Dasa at birth : years 5–3–22.

Rahu. Lord of the 9th Saturn is powerfully aspected by the maraka planet Jupiter.

Marakas for different lagnas are given in the Appendix. For further details refer to my *How to Judge a Horoscope*.

अथ विद्या विचारः

EDUCATION

शुक्रश्चतुर्थगो यस्य गानविद्या विशारदः ।
चतुर्थस्थस्सोमसुतो ज्योतिश्शास्त्र विशारदः ॥ १ ॥

Stanza 1.—If Venus is in the 4th, the person becomes proficient in music. If Mercury is in the 4th, the person becomes proficient in astrology.

रविर्वा बुधराहुर्वा पञ्चमस्थानसंस्थिताः ।
ज्योतिर्विद्याप्रवीणस्याद्विषवैद्यवरो भवेत् ॥ २ ॥

Stanza 2.—If the Sun or Mercury and Rahu be in the 5th, the native becomes learned in astrology and an expert in dealing with poisonous medicines.

द्वितीयस्थौ रविबुधौ ज्योतिर्विद्याविशारदः ।
तावेव शनिना दृष्टा गणितज्ञो भवेन्नरः ॥ ३ ॥

Stanza 3.—The person becomes well versed in astrology if the Sun and Mercury are in the 2nd. He becomes a mathematician if this combination is aspected by Saturn.

द्वितीयस्थौ रविकुजौ तर्कशास्त्रविशारदः ।
पञ्चमस्थौ मन्दभानुबुधा वेदान्तपारगः ॥ ४ ॥

Stanza 4.—If the Sun and Mars are in the 2nd the pernon becomes a logician. Saturn, Mercury and the Sun in the 5th make him well versed in philosophical knowledge.

बुधभानु केन्द्र कोण लाभस्थौ गणको भवेत् ।
द्वितीयस्थौ यदि भृगुः कविताधर्ममश्नुते ॥ ५ ॥

Stanza 5.—If Mercury and the Sun are in a Kendra, Trikona or the 11th house, the native becomes a mathematician. If Venus is in the second house he becomes a poet.

सैंहिकेयः पञ्चमस्थः गूढभावार्थवित्भवेत् ।
चतुर्थस्थ सैंहिकेयः जनन्यायुष्मती भवेत् ॥ ६ ॥

Stanza 6.—If Rahu is in the 5th, the native will be an expert in understanding the inner meaning of things. Rahu in the 4th makes the mother long-lived.

द्वितीयस्थो यदि गुर्वेदवेदांगपारगः ।
स्वोच्चस्वक्षेत्रयुक्तश्चेतभवेदेवं न संशयः ॥ ७ ॥

Stanza 7.—Jupiter in the 2nd makes the native an expert in Vedas and Vedangas. If such a 2nd house happens to be the own or exaltation place of Jupiter, the native will undoubtedly become learned as said above and,

सभापूज्यश्च संपूर्ण विद्यावान् भवति ध्रुवम् ।
वाक्स्थौ नपोवाक्पतिश्च केन्द्रकोणेषु संस्थितौ ।
सर्वविद्या प्रवीणस्तास्सभापूज्यो न संशयः ॥ ८ ॥

Stanza 8.—He will be honoured in public
assemblies. If the 2nd lord and Jupiter are placed in
a Kendra or Trikona he will be learned in different
branches of knowledge and publicly honoured.

द्वितीयस्थो यदि कुजस्तर्केशास्त्रविशारदः ।
तत्रैव च भवेदिन्दुः सूलज्ञो यजको भवेत् ॥ ९ ॥

Stanza 9.—If Mars is in the 2nd, the person
becomes learned in logic. If the Moon is also in the
2nd he will be a pandit or priest.

द्वितीयस्थो यदि भृगुः काव्यालङ्कार शास्त्रवान् ।
तत्रैवस्साद्यादि शनिर्मूढो दुष्टो भवेध्रुवम् ॥ १० ॥

Stanza 10.—Venus in the 2nd makes one learned
in Kavya (poetry) and Alankara (rhetoric). He becomes vindictive, evil-minded a and fool if Saturn is
similarly placed.

NOTES

In Sanskrit Vidya means learning and Gnana means knowledge. Knowledge is obtained not only by learning but by
deep introspection. Knowledge always refers to the knowledge of the Supreme. Being. Gnana is knowledge and writers
on yoga have tried to reconcile the view that liberation or
Moksha is attained by means of meditation with the theory that
it can be obtained by the knowledge alone. Meditation leads
to Gnana or knowledge and knowledge leads to Moksha. Here
when we refer to Vidya or learning we mean acquired know-

ledge or ideals in any branch of science or literature— erudition, knowledge acquired by experience, scholarship, experiment and observation. Knowledge on the other hand means the clear and certain perception of truth, cognition. Budha is the Karaka of Vidya (learning) while Jupiter is the Karaka of Gnana or Knowledge.

In this chapter the author gives the following combinations for proficiency in the different sciences.

Music.—Venus should be in the 4th house. Venus is the Karaka of music dancing and fine arts in general. If you examine a number of horoscopes you will find that proficiency in music can be predicted if (*a*) Venus is in the 9th or aspects the 9th house ; (*b*) if Venus is in the 5th or aspects the 5th house and (*c*) if Venus is in the 2nd or aspects the 2nd house. Interest in music may be predicted if Venus is in the 4th from the Moon. The four combinations referred to in the above paragraphs will be found in charts underneath :—

Chart No. 22. –*Born on 12–2–1856 at 12-21 p.m. L.M.T. Lat. 18° N. ; Long. 84° E.*

	Moon Rahu	Ascdt.	Sat.	Jupit.		Ascdt.	Rahu
Sun Mercury Jupiter		RASI				NAVAMSA	
				Merc.			
Venus		Mars Ketu		Ketu		Moon Sun Saturn Venus Mars	

Balance of Venus Dasa at birth : years 6–1–13.

Chart No. 23.—*Born on 7-8-1887 at 1-30 p.m., L.M.T. Lat. 11° N. ; Long. 5h. 8m. E.*

		Mars	Rahu		Mars	
Moon						
	RASI	Sun Merc Rah Sat.	Venus Sun	NAVAMSA		Moon
Ketu						
	Ascdt.	Jupiter	Venus	Jupit.	Ascdt.	Mercury	Ketu Saturn

Balance of Jupiter's Dasa at birth : years 0-7-6.

Chart No. 24.—*Born on 6/7-10-1886 at 2-20 a. m., L.M T. Lat. 13° N. ; Long. 77° 35' E.*

			Venus		Moon	
Ketu	RASI	Sat.	Ketu			Sun Saturn
Moon	III-54	Rahu Ascdt.		NAVAMSA		Jupiter Rahu Ascdt.
	Mars	Sun Merc. Jupit. Venus			Mars	Mercury

Balance of Moon's Dasa at birth : years 6-6-0.

Chart No. 25.—*Born on 8-8-1912 at 7-23 p.m., L.M.T. Lat. 13° N.; Long. 77° 35' E.*

Rahu		Saturn Moon		Saturn	Venus
Ascdt.	RASI		Sun	Rahu Sun	NAVAMSA
			Mars Merc. Venus	Ascdt.	Moon Mercury Ketu
	Jupiter		Ketu	Jupiter	Mars

Balance of Mars' Dasa at birth : years 6-0-10.

Chart No. 26.—*Born on 28-5-1903 at 1-19 a.m., L.M.T. Lat. 9° N.; Long. 77° 42' E.*

Ascdt. Ketu		Sun Moon Mercury	Venus	Mars	Venus Sun	Jupiter Saturn
Jupiter	RASI				NAVAMSA	Ascdt. Rahu
Saturn	III–8			Ketu		Moon Mercury
			Mars Rahu			

Balance of Mars' Dasa at birth :   years 5–3–25.

Astrology — (*a*) Mercury should be in the 4th, (*b*) the Sun should be in the 5th, (*c*) the Sun and Mercury should be in the 2nd.

Vedanta :— (*a*) Saturn, the Sun and Mercury should be in the 5th, (*b*) Jupiter should be in the 2nd to be learned in Vedas and their Angas.

Veda is different from Vedanta. I do not propose to say anything about the delicate differences existing between Veda and Vedanta in the course of these notes. I am fully aware of my incapacity to deal with such profound ideas. Vedas are the repository of knowledge while Vedanta begins where Veda ends. A glimpse of Vedanta philosophy can be had by going through the famous Brahma Sutras of Badarayana. After having obtained a knowledge of karmas prescribed in the Vedas and having known that their results cannot give everlasting bliss and a time comes when a person becomes indifferent to karmas, and therefore naturally a desire arises in him for the knowledge of Brahma. WHO is above *Karma* and WHO is the source of everlasting bliss ? Vedanta gives the knowledge of the Supreme Being.

Stanza 4 gives combinations for proficiency in Vedanta while Stanza 7 deals with proficiency in Vedas and Vedangas. For understanding the Vedas properly, a thorough knowledge of the angas or auxiliaries, *viz*, *Siksha*, *Vyakarana*, *Niruktha*, *Chandas*, *Tarka* and *Jyotisha* is essential. Astrology is an Upaveda and therefore its study is highly esteemed by the ancient writers.

Poet : One becomes a poet if the 2nd house is occupied by Venus. In *Chart No.* 27 Venus is in the 2nd with Mercury and the Sun is exalted. This is the horoscope of one of the greatest poets of our time. Venus is lord of the 3rd and the

Chart No. 27.—*Born on 7-5-1861 at 4-2 a.m.
Lat. 22° 40' N. ; Long. 88° 30' E.*

Ascdt Moon	Sun Mercury Venus		Mars Ketu	Jupit. Ascdt.		Ketu	Mercury
			Jupit.				Saturn
	RASI 4-83			NAVAMSA			
			Sat.	Moon			
Rahu				Venus Sun Rahu		Mars	

Balance of Mercury's Dasa at birth :   years 9-5-22.

8th   The evil due to this circumstance may find expression in
different forms but the fact of the presence of Venus in the 2nd
gave the native great poetical powers.

Diplomat.—Stanza 6 says that if Rahu is in the 5th the
native will know the inner meaning of things.   He probes into
the minds of others and tries to understand their mental
currents.   In other words, he will be a diplomat to the core.
Of course diplomacy is only a dignified term for concealed
hypocrisy.   Personally I feel that one becomes a diplomat even
if Rahu aspects the 5th house.

If Mars is in the 2nd, one becomes a logician.   All people
cannot become logicians in the strict sense.   So it may be said
that one who has Mars posited in or aspecting the 2nd becomes
clever in arguments.   Chart No. 28 furnishes a good illustration.   Mark Rahu aspecting the 5th and Mars aspecting the
2nd.   Stanza 10 says that if Saturn is in the 2nd, the person

becomes vindictive and violent. This combination is also present because Saturn aspects the 2nd but his evil is greatly tempered as the 2nd is also aspected by Jupiter. All-round learning can be predicted if Jupiter is in the 2nd or aspects the 2nd without any malefic aspects.

Chart No. 28.—*Born on 16–10–1918 at 2–26 p.m. I S.T. Lat. 13° N. ; Long. 77° 35′ E.*

		Ketu	Jupit.			Saturn Jupiter	
Moon					Rahu		Venus
	RASI HJH–12				NAVAMSA		
Ascdt.			Sat.	Moon			Ketu
	Mars Rahu	Mercury Sun	Venus	Mars		Mercury Sun	Ascdt.

Balance of Rahu's Dasa at birth : years 11-8-20.

अथ भुक्ति विचारः

ON TASTES OR FLAVOURS

तृतीयस्थो भवेन्मन्दः तृतीयेशयुतोऽपि वा ।
पश्यन्नपि तृतीयं च कटुवाम्लद्रव्यभुक्भवेत् ॥ १ ॥

Stanza 1.—If Saturn is in the 3rd or he is combined with the lord of the 3rd, or aspects the 3rd, the person likes pungent and sour flavours.

तृतीये तु स्थितो भौमः उष्णद्रव्यप्रियो भवेत् ।
तत्र स्थितो वाक्पतिश्चेत्सात्विक द्रव्य भुक्भवेत् ॥ २ ॥

Stanza   2.—If Mars is in the 3rd, the person likes hot things.   If Jupiter is in the 3rd, he likes Satvik foods.

द्वितीये यदि शुक्रस्य तांबूलादिप्रियो भवेत् ।
व्यभिचार रतश्चासीत्तत्स्थो यदि भार्गवः ॥ ३ ॥

Stanza   3.—If Venus is in the 2nd the person will be addicted to chewing betels and will have loose morals.

द्वितीयस्थो यदि शनिर्मन्दवाग्लौभ्यवान् भवेत् ।
द्वितीयस्थो केतु गुरु वा चतु निपुणो भवेत् ॥ ४ ॥

Stanza   4.—If Saturn is in the 2nd, the native speaks rudely and indistinctly.   If Ketu or Jupiter is there, he will be a clever speaker.

भानु भौमौ द्वियीयस्थौ वाक्षुकाठिन्यमुच्यते ।
द्वितीये संस्थितश्चेन्दुवक्छु संभ्रम उच्यते ॥ ५ ॥

Stanza   5.—If the Sun and Mars are in the 2nd, the person will be harsh in his speech.   If the Moon is there, he will be very talkative.

द्वितीयस्थस्सोमसुतो युक्तियुक्तं वचो भवेत् ।
तत्रैव संस्थितो राहुः वाक्षुद्दीनन्वमुच्यते ॥ ६ ॥

Stanza 6.—If Mercury is in the 2nd, he will talk cleverly and skilfully. If on the other hand Rahu is there humility will characterise his behaviour.

द्वितीयस्थो यदि कविः क्षीरभक्ष्यादि शुक्रभवेत् ।
तत्रस्थो राहु केतू वै समयोचित शुक्रभवेत् ॥ ७ ॥

Stanza 7.—If Venus is in the 2nd, the native consumes milk and varieties of dishes. If Rahu or Ketu is there he will eat food according to circumstances.

द्वितीयस्थोयदि शनिः शूद्रान्नं कुत्सितो धनम् ।
उच्छिष्टान्नं च श्राद्धान्नं जातोह्यात्ति न संशयः ॥ ८ ॥

Stanza 8.—If Saturn is in the 2nd, the native gets food polluted by Sudras, remnants of food left by others and food prepared at the times of obsequies and death ceremonies.

NOTES

In this chapter the author deals with the tastes or flavours liked by different persons born with different planetary combinations. The Hindus had long ago realised that flavours or *rasas* developed human nature in certain channels. According to Ayurveda there are six important Rasas, *viz.,* sweet (*madhuram*), sour (*amla*), saline (*lavana*), pungent (*khara*), bitter (*kahi*), astringent (*kashaya*) These shadrasas (six kinds of flavours) play an important part in the classification and distribution of the food after it is taken in. Sweet is nutritive and rejuvenating. It has a cooling property. It predisposes to wounds, urinary disorders and enlargements of glands in the body. Sour increases saliva and appetite for food. With

saline ducts of the body are purified. Pungent produces a
burning sensation on the tongue. It clears and purifies the
ducts of the body. Thus each flavour has certain properties
helping in the digestion of the food. If certain planets are
disposed in a certain manner, the individual takes liking for
certain flavours and his temperament and mental disposition
largely depend upon the likes and dislikes he shows towards
the different flavours.

People who are emotional and short-tempered like pungent foods. Intellectuals like sour foods and so on. There
are of course exceptions. According to astrological termino-
logy planetary relations of the different rasas are as follows :—

Planet		Rasa		Flavour
The Sun	....	Khara	...	Pungent
The Moon	...	Lavana	...	Saline or Saltish
Mars	....	Kahi	....	Bitter
Mercury	....	Misram	....	Mixed
Jupiter	....	Madhuram	....	Sweet
Venus	....	Amla	....	Sour
Saturn	....	Kashayam	....	Astringent

There seems to be some difference between our author
and other ancient writers on astrology in the matter of allo-
cation of the Rasas. According to this book if Saturn is in the
3rd from the Ascendant or is in conjunction with the 3rd lord
or aspects the 3rd, the person likes pungent and acid flavours.
The Sun rules pungent things while Venus rules sour things.
Of course only one combination is given here and this, as I have
observed, holds good in a number of horoscopes. It is incom-
plete and therefore readers have to attempt predictions by
taking into account the allotment of flavours as given above.

The person eats Satvik foods if Jupiter is in the 3rd (stanza 2). Different kinds of food develop different natures in men. No one can deny that climatic influences, environmental factors and the foods we eat direct our mental currents in particular channels and develop our natures in different ways. According to astrology, the Sun, the Moon and Jupiter are divine in nature and indicate Satvika guna or a philosophic disposition. Venus and Mercury represent Rajasa or imperious disposition ; Mars and Saturn denote Thamsa or mild nature.

Take a person addicted to drinks and luxurious forms of meals. He will certainly be *Rajasa*. Take a person who likes simple food and avoids all forms of luxuries and harmful dishes. His disposition will be entirely different. All these differences can be easily ascertained by a careful study of the planetary dispositions in the horoscope.

When the author says in stanzas 2 and 3 that the person likes Satvik foods if Jupiter is in the 3rd and that he will be loose in morals if Venus is in the 2nd, it is full of significance and should enable the intelligent reader to anticipate how the temperament of an individual stands when other planets are situated in the 2nd and 3rd houses.

The creative energy called *Prakrithi* manifested itself in three different forms producing different characters in the being in whom they are indicated. Satvika (indicated by Jupiter, the Sun and the Moon) is pure and causes light and knowledge. It produces happiness and wisdom, faith and love. Rajasa (ruled by Venus and Mercury) denotes desires for objects and binds the soul by the chords of passionate wants. Thamasa (ruled by Mars and Saturn) makes all people avaricious and causes laziness, negligence and evil inclinations. Satva gives moral happiness, Rajasa makes one proud and

vain. Thamasa makes one bad and do evil work. The concen-
tration of mind and its elevation depend upon the influences of
the planets, which obtain an ascendancy at the time of birth.
Planets indicate what sort of nature a man possesses. If in a
man Thamasa and Rajasa predominate, provided planets
denoting these respective characteristics are powerful, then by
proper regulation of the external influences surrounding him
on Sastraic ordinances it is possible to produce desirable
mental characteristics and make men Satvikas. It is on this
principle that regulations in diet, in sleep, in occupations, in
sexual relations and in mental outlook are laid down by the
Hindu sages.

Stanzas 5 and 6 reveal whether a man would be talkative,
whether his speech would be harsh or plesant and whether he
could talk clearly or indistinctly and so on.

Ketu, Jupiter and Mercury in the 2nd are good while the
Sun, Mars and Saturn make one harsh in his speech and
behaviour. Rahu in the 2nd makes one humble in his addresses.
In other words, humility will characterise his behaviour. Some
say that humility is a virtue in as much as it denotes absence
of egoism and self-importance. Some mistake humility for
cowardice. But such men are themselves mistaken. One
important fact should be noted. Saturn in the 2nd is undesir-
able because it makes one mean, harsh, undignified, lacking
self-respect, quick-tempered and foul-tongued. Of course these
results should not be predicted if the evil influences are relieved
by the conjunctions and aspects of natural benefics—particularly Jupiter and Venus.

Thus ends the Second Chapter entitled "Wealth and
Education" in *Bhavartha Ratnakara* of Sri Ramanujacharya.

CHAPTER III

अथ भ्रातृयोगतरङ्गः

BROTHERS

अभ्रातृस्थानेश्वरस्याषि भ्रातृणां कारकेण वै ।
कुजेन सह संबन्ध भ्रातृवृद्धिरुदीरिता ॥ १ ॥

Stanza 1.—The existence of brothers should be divined either from the lord of the 3rd or from the karaka of brothers or from the planets combined with Mars.

विक्रमे विक्रमाधीश रविभूमिसुतास्थिताः ।
भवेद्यदि हि जातस्तु साहसी धीर उच्यते ॥ २ ॥

Stanza 2.—One becomes brave and courageous if the lord of the 3rd, the Sun and Mars are in the 3rd house.

राहुकेतू तृतीयस्थौ जातस्साहसिको भवेत् ।
तलैव स्यास्सोमसुतो धैर्यंहीनो भवेन्नरः ॥ ३ ॥

Stanza 3.—The person becomes brave if the 3rd is occupied by Rahu and Ketu. He will be timid if Mercury is in the 3rd.

बलहीने भ्रातृभावे संबन्धो गुरुभौमयो: ।

अस्तिचेत्भ्रातृ बहुल वक्तव्यं विबुधोत्तमे: ॥ ४ ॥

Stanza   4.—If the 3rd house being weak is occupied or aspected by Jupiter and Mars, the native will
have brothers.

लाभस्थो यदि देवेज्य: ज्येष्ठभ्रातुस्तु दु:खद: ।

लाभे च संस्थितो भौम: शनिना वीक्षितो यदि ॥ ५ ॥

Stanza   5.—The person suffers sorrow from elder
brother if Jupiter is in the 11th.   If Mars is in the same
position aspected by Saturn.

भ्रातृणां ज्येष्ठसंज्ञानां ह्यभाव: प्रोच्यते बुधै: ।

षष्ठाष्टमे भ्रातृधीश: भ्रातारिष्टं तु कथ्यते ॥ ६ ॥

Stanza   6.—The person will not have an elder
brother.   If the 3rd lord is in the 6th or the 8th, death
of brothers will happen.

क्षत्रियाणां जातकेतु राज्येशो विक्रमे यदि ।

राजयोगस्य न्यूनं हि भवत्येव न संशय: ॥ ७ ॥

Stanza   7.—Destruction of Rajayoga will occur if
(in the horoscopes of kings and rulers) the 10th lord is
in the 3rd.

धनादिपतिना भ्रातृनायकस्य सहस्थिति: ।

औदार्यंतस्य वक्तव्यं जातकस्य बुधोत्तमे: ॥ ८ ॥

Stanza 8.—The learned in astrology predict generous instincts if the 3rd lord is combined with the 2nd lord.

धन भ्रातृपतिभ्यां वा संबन्धस्सूर्यंजस्य हि ।
बहुलौभ्यं हि वक्तव्यं जातकस्य सदा बुधैः ॥ ९ ॥

Stanza 9.—Professors in astrology say that the person becomes a miser if Saturn is combined with the 2nd and 3rd lords.

षष्ठाष्टमव्यये भ्रातृनायको यदि संस्थितः ।
तत्रैव शुभसंयुक्ते ह्यरिष्टं तु चिरादभवेत् ॥ १० ॥

Stanza 10.—If the lord of the 3rd is in the 6th, the 8th or the 12th, death of brothers will take place. If benefics are in these houses, then death (of brothers) will take place late in life.

NOTES

The 3rd house rules brothers, sisters and courage while the 11th rules elder brothers. The stanzas are simple and are easily understandable. Mercury's presence in the 3rd makes one timid and funky while he becomes brave and courageous when the 3rd is occupied by Mars and the Sun. The presence of Rahu and Ketu in the 3rd is also suggestive of bravery and courage. If the 3rd lord is combined with the 2nd lord, the native will possess generous instincts. If Saturn is connected with the 2nd and 3rd lords, the person becomes a miser.

Stanza 1, 5, 6 and 10 deal with brothers. The 3rd is the house of brothers and Mars is *Bhratrukaraka*. The presence of brothers should be ascertained from (a) the lord of the 3rd,

(b) Mars, and (c) the planet in conjunction with (or aspected by) Mars. If the 3rd house is weak but is combined with or aspected by Mars and Jupiter, the native will have brothers.

Chart No. 29 :—*Born on 24-8-1880 at Gh. 37-10 after sunrise. Lat. 13° N. ; Long. 77° 35' E.*

Ascdt.	Rahu	Ketu Jupiter	
		Moon Merc.	Sun
	RASI	NAVAMSA	
Jupiter	III-59	Sun Sat.	Mars	Saturn Venus
	Moon Mars Ketu	Merc. Venus	Ascdt.	Rahu

Balance of Mercury's Dasa at birth : years 7-3-24.

In Chart No. 29 the 3rd house is occupied by Rahu, a malefic and aspected by Saturn. This suggests that the 3rd house is weak. But note that both Mars and Jupiter are aspecting the 3rd house. This is indicative of the presence of a number of brothers and sisters (stanza 4). Jupiter is in the 11th from the Ascendant. The 11th rules elder brother as per stanza 5 ; the native has an elder brother from whom no benefits is derived. Rahu in the 3rd has made the person quite courageous (stanza 3).

Taking Chart No. 30 Ketu is in the 3rd house and hence the 3rd Bhava is vitiated. Mars aspects the 3rd as also the Sun, Mercury, Rahu and Saturn. Ketu in the 3rd gives the

Chart No 30:—*Born on 7–8–1887 at 1–21 p.m. (L.M.T.)
Lat. 11° N. ; Long. 5h. 8m. E.*

Moon			Mars	Rahu		Mars	
			Sun Merc. Rahu Sat.	Sun Venus			Moon
	RASI				NAVAMSA		
Ketu							
	Ascdt.	Jupiter	Venus	Jupit.		Ascdt. Mercury	Ketu Saturn

Balance of Jupiter's Dasa at birth : years 0–8–5.

person courage and the partial blemish of the 3rd house is over-
come by Mars aspecting the 3rd. The native has a brother.

In the horoscopes of rulers (stanza 2) if the 10th lord is
in the 3rd, the Raja Yoga becomes defunct.

Thus ends the Third Chapter entitled "Brothers" in
Bhavartha Ratnakara of Sri Ramanujacharya.

CHAPTER IV

अथ वाहनयोगातरङ्गः

CONVEYANCES AND FORTUNE

भाग्येशो वाहनेशश्च ताबुभौ लग्नगौ यदि ।
भाग्यबाहन योगोऽयमित्याहुर्गणकोत्तमाः ॥ १ ॥

Stanza 1.—Astrologers say that the person possesses fortune and vehicles if the lords of the 4th and the 9th combine together in the Ascendant.

सुखस्थानं गतो वापि पश्यन्नपि गुरुर्यदि ।
बहुसौख्यमवाप्नोति जातस्तत्र न संशयः ॥ २ ॥

Stanza 2.—The native will undoubtedly be extremely happy if Jupiter occupies or aspects the 4th house.

चतुर्थेश गुरु यत्र केन्द्रकोणेषु संगतौ ।
स्थितौ चत्सुखमाप्नोति जातस्तत्र न संशयः ॥ ३ ॥

Stanza 3.—There is no doubt that the person enjoys happiness if Jupiter and lord of the 4th combine in a Kendra or a Trikona.

NOTES

In the modern world every one aspires to possess a motor car – the 20th century *vahana*. Stanza 1 says that if the lords of the Ascendant and the 9th are in the Ascendant, the native will not only be fortunate but will also command conveyances. We shall come to this point subsequently. Stanzas 2 and 3 deal with happiness. Happiness is an elusive term. The poor man feels that the rich man is happy. A childless man feels that one with children is happy and so on. Happiness must be judged relatively. That is, taking into account, the law of compensation one may be declared to be generally happy if he commands conveniences for leading a decent and honourable life, has a loving wife, affectionate children and some name and fame. Man cannot achieve *absolute* happiness because, in the final analysis, absolute happiness is only a state of mind that can be reached by deep meditation and a completely detached attitude of life. If Jupiter aspects the 4th or is posited there, the native will be happy (stanza 2) as also when Jupiter and lord of the 4th house are placed in a quadrant or trine (stanza 3). Some scholars opine that according to stanza 3, Jupiter should own the 4th house. Jupiter owning a Kendra is bad but if he is in a Kendra or Trikona his malefic nature obtained temporarily might either be counteracted or, it might find manifestation in other ways.

In the following horoscope (Chart No. 31) Jupiter aspects the 4th, as also lords of the 4th and the 5th. Of course Saturn also aspects the 4th. Though the native had all the worries and woes which every human being has, and will have, Jupiter aspecting the 4th gave him that inner happiness which made him impervious to all outer distractions. He felt really happy and he was justified in this claim that he was quite happy.

Chart No. 31.—*Born on 12-2-1856 at 21-21 p.m L.M.T. Lat. 18° N. ; Long. 84° E.*

Moon Rahu	Ascdt.	Sat.	Jupit.		Ascdt.	Rahu
Sun Mercury Jupiter	RASI			NAVAMSA		
			Merc.			
Venus	Mars Ketu		Ketu		Sun Saturn Venus Mars	

Balance of Venus' Dasa at birth : years 12-3-9.

वाहनेशेन संयुक्तः कारको वाहनस्य तु ।
एकौ स्थितौ वाहनेचेत् खलपवाहनमुच्यते ॥ ४ ॥

Stanza 4.—If Venus is in the 4th with the lord of the 4th the person will possess ordinary conveyances.

वाहनाधिप शुक्रौ तु लाभे वा भाग्यसेपि वा ।
राज्ये वा संस्थितौ वाऽपि वाहन प्रबलप्रदौ ॥ ५ ॥

Stanza 5.—If Venus as lord of the 4th is in the 11th or the 9th or the 10th, the native will possess a number of conveyances.

वाहनाधिपतेर्येस्तु संबन्धो विधुना यदि ।
अश्ववाहनयोगोऽयमित्युक्तो गणिकोत्तमैः ॥ ६ ॥

Stanza 6.—If the 4th lord is connected with the Moon, astrologers predict possession of carriages drawn by horses.

बुधशुक्रौ चतुर्थे तु कर्कि जातस्य संस्थितौ ।
बुधदाये भृगोरन्तर्दशायां वाहनं भवेत् ॥ ७ ॥

Stanza 7.—A person born in Cancer, with Mercury and Venus in the 4th, will acquire conveyances in Mercury Dasa Venus Bhukti.

NOTES

The above four stanzas deal with the circumstances under which a man will be able to possess conveyances. The author has necessarily been brief but the combinations enable us to extend the principles further so that they may be applied to any number of horoscopes. *Vahanakaraka* is Venus and *Vahanasthana* is the 4th. His favourable disposition indicates acquisition of vehicles.

If the 4th lord is connected with the Moon, the subject will have horse-drawn carriages. In Chart No. 32, which belongs to a Maharaja, there is interchange of houses between the 1st and 4th lords. The native had a number of vahanas —moter cars, horses, horse-drawn carriages, palanquins, etc. Take a number of horoscopes and study them in the light of the above principles.

अश्ववाहनकर्तास्यार्श्चतुर्थस्थो गुह्मभवेत् ।
सप्तमस्थे भवेच्छुक्रः अतिकामुक उच्यते ॥ ८ ॥

Stanza 8.—If Jupiter is in the 4th, the native will possess horses and horse-drawn carriages. If Venus is in the 7th, he will become very sensual.

चतुर्थेख्याद्यदि शनिः परदेशेन वसत्यसौ ।

छिद्रग्रहेषु वसति काठिन्यहृदयो भवेत् ॥ ९ ॥

Stanza 9.—If Saturn is in the 4th, the person lives in foreign countries. He will live in old and dilapidated houses and will be hard-hearted.

Chart No. 32.— *Born on 4-6-1884 at 10-18 a.m., Lat. 12° N.; Long. 76° 38' E.*

Ketu		Sun Saturn Mercury		Ascdt Ketu		Mars
		Ascdt. Jupit. Venus				Sun Venus Saturn
RASI HJH-12				NAVAMSA		
		Mars	Merc.			
	Moon	Rahu			Moon Jupiter	Rahu

Balance of Mars' Dasa at birth : years 1–11–12.

NOTES

In Chart No. 31 Jupiter is powerfully aspecting the 4th. The native maintained an excellent dog cart in the early years of this century.

In Chart No. 25 Venus is in the 7th. The native is passionate but his passions will not be ill-spent as Jupiter is in
the 10th or house of Karma besides Mercury being in the 7th.
Saturn has the power of doing mischief in various ways. But
he will give the person in the end great fortitude, patience and
forbearance. Saturn's presence in the 4th not only spoils the
indications of the 4th house but also makes the native unhappy. These evil results should not be predicted if Saturn in
the 4th is in conjunction with or aspected by benefics particularly Jupiter and Venus and if he also happens to be lord of
the Ascendant or the Moon sign.

वाहनाधिपतिर्भाग्ये भाग्येशो वाहने यदि ।
भाग्यवाहन योगोऽयमिति तज्ञा वदन्ति हि ॥ १० ॥

Stanza 10.—The learned in astrology say that
a person will have Bhagyavahana Yoga, if lords of the
4th and the 9th interchange their houses.

वाहनाधिपतिर्लाभे लाभेशो वाहने यदि ।
भाग्यवाहन योगोऽयमिति तज्ञा वदन्ति हि ॥ ११ ॥

Stanza 11.—Astrologers predict Bhagyavahana
Yoga if the 4th lord is in the 11th and the 11th lord is
in the 4th.

वाहनेशः पञ्चमस्य: पञ्चमे वाहनाधिप: ।
भाग्यवाहन योगोयऽमिति तज्ञा वदन्ति हि ॥ १२ ॥

Stanza 12.—Similar results occur if the 4th and
5th lords interchange their places.

वाहनाधिपतिर्लग्ने लग्नेशो वाहने यदि ।
भाग्यवाहन योगोऽयमितिस्त्यूचुर्गणकोत्तमाः ॥ १३ ॥

Stanza 13.—The learned in astrology predict Bhagyavahana Yoga if lords of the Ascendant and the 4th interchange their places.

पञ्चमाधिपतिर्भांग्ये भाग्येशः पञ्चमे यदि ।
भाग्यवाहन योगोऽयमति तज्ज्ञा वदन्ति हि ॥ १४ ॥

Stanza 14.—The learned in astrology say that Bhagyavahana Yoga is caused if the 5th lord is in the 9th and the 9th lord is in the 5th.

पञ्चमाधिपतिर्लाभे पञ्चमस्थो हि लाभपः ।
भाग्यवाहन योगोऽयमिति तज्ज्ञा वदन्ति हि ॥ १५ ॥

Stanza 15.—Astrologers say that Bhagyavahana Yoga is caused if the 5th lord is in the 11th and the 11th lord is in the 5th.

वाहनेशो वाहनस्थः पञ्चमे पञ्चमेश्वरः ।
भाग्यवाहन योगोऽयमिति तज्ज्ञा वदन्ति हि ॥ १६ ॥

Stanza 16.—Similar results will occur if lords of the 4th and the 5th are in their respective houses.

भाग्याधिपो भाग्यस्यात् लग्नेशो लग्नगो यदि ।
भाग्यवाहन योगोऽयमिति तज्ज्ञा वदन्ति हि ॥ १७ ॥

Stanza 17.—Similar results should be predicted if lords of the 9th and the Ascendant are in their respective houses.

पञ्चमाधिपतिभांग्ये राज्ये वा भाग्यनायक: ।
भाग्यवाहन योगोऽयमिति तज्ज्ञा वदन्ति हि ॥ १८ ॥

Stanza 18.—The learned in astrology predict Bhagyavahana Yoga if the 5th lord is in the 9th and the 9th lord is in the 10th.

NOTES

Bhagyavahana Yoga simply means a combination which ensures the general fortune of the native and gives him at the same time possession of conveyances and similar comforts. The combinations given in stanzas 10 to 18 are no more than ordinary Raja Yogas in which lords of certain (benefic) houses exchange their places with other (benefic) houses. In other words, they are all *Subhaparivarthana Yogas* and they do not need any elucidation. However, I shall summarise them for ready reference of the reader.

The person gets vehicles and his general fortune is assured by the following combinations :-

1. Lord of 4 in 9 and lord of 9 in 4.
2. Lord of 4 in 11 and lord of 11 in 4.
3. Lord of 4 in 5 and lord of 5 in 4.
4. Lord of 4 in 1 and lord of 1 in 4.
5. Lord of 5 in 9 and lord of 9 in 5.
6. Lord of 5 in 11 and lord of 11 in 5.
7. Lord of 9 in 9 and lord of 1 in 1.
8. Lord of 5 in 9 and lord of 9 in 10.

By a certain interchange of positions between lords of 11 and 9, 4 and 5, 4 and 1, 5 and 9, 4 and 5, 5 and 9, 5 and 11, 9 and 10 various *Bhagyavahana Yogas* are formed.

पञ्चमस्याधिपतिना संबन्धो यदि विद्यते ।
पुलकारक जीवस्य पुलप्राबल्यमादिशेत् ॥ १९ ॥

Stanza 19.—Birth of children must be predicted if Jupiter and the 5th lord are in mutual conjunction or aspect.

पुलकारक पुलेश लग्नेशाः केन्द्रकोणगाः ।
पुलसौख्यमवाप्नोति जातस्तत्र न संशयः ॥ २० ॥

Stanza 20.—The native will positively enjoy happiness from children if Jupiter, lord of the 5th and lord of Ascendant are disposed in Kendras and Trikonas.

Chart No. 33, —*Born on 8-8-1912 at 7-23 p.m (L.M.T.) Lat. 13° N ; Long. 77° 35' E.*

Rahu	Saturn Moon			Saturn	Venus
Ascdt.	RASI	Sun — Mars Merc. Venus	Rahu Sun — Ascdt.	NAVAMSA	Moon Mercury Ketu
	Jupitr	Ketu		Jupiter	Mars

Balance of Mars' Dasa at birth : years 6-0-10.

NOTES

The author has been very brief with regard to the 5th house having included it along with the treatment of the 4th house. The native will have children and happiness on their account if lords of the Ascendant and the 5th and Jupiter are in trines and quadrants.

In Chart No. 33 lord of the Ascendant is Saturn, lord of the 5th is Mercury and Putrakaraka is Jupiter. Readers will see that all these three planets are in Kendras suggesting that the native will have a number of children and also happiness through them.

Thus ends the Fourth Chapter entitled "Conveyances and Fortune" in *Bhavartha Ratnakara* of Sri Ramanujacharya.

CHAPTER V

अथ शत्रुरोगादि तरङ्गः

ENEMIES AND DISEASES

अष्टमाधिपतौ लग्ने रोगदेहो भवेन्नरः ।
षष्ठेशे लग्नगे वाऽपि ज्ञाति रोगौश्च बाध्यते ॥ १ ॥

Stanza 1.—If the lord of the 8th is in the 1st, the person will have a sickly body. If the lord of the 6th is in the Ascendant, he will be troubled by cousins and diseases.

अग्रषष्ठाधिपाभ्यान्तु सूर्यचन्द्रमसौ युतौ ।
भानुना ण्वरगण्डस्याच्चन्द्रेण जलगण्डकम् ॥ २ ॥

Stanza 2.—If the Sun and the Moon are combined with the lords of the 1st and the 6th, the person will have fear from fever and fear from water, respectively.

कुजेन व्रणशस्त्रादि ग्रन्थि रोगभयं भवेत् ।
बुधेन संगतौस्यातां पित्तरोगी भवेन्नरः ॥ ३ ॥

Stanza 3.—If Mars is with lords of the Ascendant and the 6th, the person suffers from wounds, weapons and plague. If Mercury is similarly disposed, he will suffer from diseases due to bile.

देवेन्द्रपूज्य संयोगे रोगाभाव उद्दीरितः ।
शनिना यदि योगोऽयं चोरचण्डालजं भयं ॥ ४ ॥

Stanza   4.—If Jupiter is similarly conjoined, the
native suffers from no diseases. If Saturn is similarly
combined, he will have fear from thieves and low-class
people.

राहुणा केतुना वापि संयोगो यदि विद्यते ।
जातस्य सर्पव्याघ्रादि भयं चाहुर्मनीषिणः ॥ ५ ॥

Stanza   5.—If Rahu and Ketu are in conjunction
with lords of the Ascendant and the 6th, the native
will have fear from reptiles and feline animals.

शुक्रेण सहसंयोगे कलत्रविपदं भवेत् ।
विक्रमेश युते भौमे युद्धान्निधनमुच्यते ॥ ६ ॥

Stanza   6.—If Venus is with lords of the Ascendant and the 6th, danger to wife is shown. If the lord
of the 3rd and Mars join together, he will die in war.

रोगाधिपे व्यवस्थे तु नीचादिग्रहसंयुते ।
लग्नेशे बलसंयुक्ते रोगनाशं वदेद्बुधः ॥ ७ ॥

Stanza   7.—If the 8th lord is in the 12th in
combination with debilitated or inimical planets and
the lord of the Ascendant is strong, the person's
diseases will all be destroyed.

बलहीने लग्ननाथाच्छत्रुस्थानाधिपे यदि ।
शुभग्रहैश्च संबन्धे शत्रुमैलं समा दिशेत् ॥ ८ ॥

Stanza   8.— If the lord of the Ascendant happening also to be lord of the 6th, is weak but is combined with benefic planets, the native's enemies will turn friends.

NOTES

In this chapter the author briefly deals with diseases and debts. The presence of the 8th lord in the Ascendant is not recommended as also that of the 6th in the Ascendant. In the first case the native will always suffer from disease while in the 2nd instance he will suffer not only from physical diseases but his mind will be worried due to the machinations of cousins and other relatives.   The author has not made any reference to the results that would be produced if the Ascendant is aspected by the 6th and (or) 8th lord or the Ascendant is associated with or aspected by these two lords.   Probably he wants us to anticipate the results.

In the annexed horoscope (*Chart No. 34*) lord of the 8th aspects the Ascendant and lord of the 6th is associated with lord of the Ascendant. The latter evil is greatly minimised because Jupiter powerfully aspects both Saturn and the Moon. As lord of the 8th aspects the Ascendant, the native looks somewhat sickly.

Danger from fever is indicated, according to stanza 2, if the Sun is in conjunction with both the lords of the Ascendant and the 6th. Similarly danger from water should be foretold if the 1st and the 6th lords are with the Moon. If supposing the 6th lord happens to be either the Sun or the Moon (in case of Aquarius and Pisces), then danger from the two sources mentioned above should not be predicted. Similarly if the 1st and

Chart No. 34.— *Born on 8-8-1912 at 7-23 p.m. (L.M.T.)*
Lat. 13° N. ; Long. 77° 35' E.

Rahu		Saturn Moon			Saturn	Venus
Ascdt.			Sun	Rahu Sun		
	RASI		Mars Merc. Venus	Ascdt.	NAVAMSA	Moon Mercury Ketu
	Jupiter		Ketu		Jupiter	Mars

Balance of Mars' Dasa at birth : years 6–0–10.

6th lords are cambined with Mars, there will be danger from
wounds. weapons and *grandhiroga* (a disease like plague). If
Mercury joins the combination of the 1st and 6th lords ; the
native suffers from bilious troubles. If Jupiter joins, there will
be no diseases. If Saturn joins this combination, there will be
trouble from thieves ang low-class persons. If Rahu and Ketu
join the combination, the person will have from reptiles and
animals of the Felis genus such as lions, tigers, etc. If Venus
joins the combination, danger to wife is indicated. The person
will die in battle if the 3rd lord joins Mars (Stanza 6). So far
as the combination in stanza 6 is concerned, the student
must use much discretion before venturing a prediction. If the
3rd lord happens to be Mars, then the combination becomes
ineffective.

The author stress the fact that to possess good health the lord of the Ascendant should be well placed while the 8th lord should be as weak as possible

The last stanza is important. According to it even enemies become friends if lord of the Ascendant is weak but happens to be lord of the 6th also and is well aspected and conjoined. This is possible in respect of Taurus and Scorpio Ascendants as Venus and Mars can become lords of the Ascendant and the 6th. The combinations are certainly thought-provoking and give much food for reflective minds.

Thus ends the Fifth Chapter, entitled "Enemies and Debts" in *Bhavartha Ratnakara* of Sri Ramanujacharya.

CHAPTER VI

अथ कळकामुक तरङ्गः

SEVENTH HOUSE INDICATIONS

कळलाधिपतिर्ग्रस्तु कारकेण युतो यदि ।
क्रूरसंबन्ध रहितः कळलं चैकमेव हि ॥ १ ॥

Stanza 1.—If the lord of the 7th is combined with Venus and has no malefic aspects or conjunctions, the person will have only one marriage.

पापग्रहस्य संबन्धः कळलाधिपते यदि ।
कुटुंबे सप्तमे वापि स्थिताः पापग्रहा यदि ॥ २ ॥

Stanza 2.—If the lord of the 7th is combined with malefics and malefics are in the 2nd and the 7th,

लाभे गतो वा शुक्रश्च शुक्रो नीचं गतोऽपि वा ।
सप्तमाधिपतिष्ठे व्यये वा संस्थितो यदि ॥ ३ ॥

Stanza 3.—If Venus occupied the 11th or is debilitated ; if the 7th lord is in the 6th or in the 12th,

कळलान्तरयोगोयं विद्वद्भिः परिकीर्तितः ।
लग्ने पापग्रहयुते कळलान्तरभाक् भवेत् ॥ ४ ॥

Stanza 4.—The native will have more than one wife. If malefics are in the Ascendant, then also the native will have more than one wife.

कुटुंबदाररन्ध्रेषु चतुर्थे व्ययमेऽपि वा ।
सितः कुजश्च शुक्रश्च बलहीनो द्विदारदः ॥ ५ ॥

Stanza 5.—If Saturn, Mars and Venus are weak and occupy the 2nd, the 7th, the 8th, the 4th and the 12th, the person will have two wives.

कुटुंबसप्ताष्टमवाहनन्यये॓ऽवस्थितोभूमिसुतस्तथैवा ।
देवेन्द्रपूज्यस्तु गुरुः कुटुंबे चिरात्कलान्तर-
                              मादिशांति ॥ ६ ॥

Stanza 6.—Similar results have to be predicted if Mars is in the 2nd, the 7th, the 8th, the 4th and the 12th. If Jupiter is in the 2nd, the person will have a second wife late in life.

शनिः कुटुंबे राहुश्चेत्सप्तमे यदि विद्यते ।
द्विकलत्रकयोगोयमित्याहुर्जातकोविदाः ॥ ७ ॥

Stanza 7.—Astrologers say that a person will have two marriages if Saturn is in the 2nd or Rahu is in the 7th.

NOTES

In stanza 1 the author says that if the 7th lord and Venus are free from affliction, the person will have only one marriage. In the next six stanzas combinations are given for two marriages. Whenever, in the course of translation, reference

is made to more than one wife it should be taken to mean
more than. one marriage. It also implies a second marriage
after the death of the first wife. The stanzas are simple enough
and need no explanation at all. One important principle seems
to emerge out from the above stanzas and that is the less the
7th lord and Venus are afflicted, the less will be the misery
and cares arising from the 7th house indications. The 2nd
house is equally important because it represents *Kutumba* or
family. Thus in order to have a smooth sailing in all affairs
connected with family and wife both the 2nd and the 7th,
their lords and Venus, should be properly fortified.

द्वितीयासप्तमेशौनु शुक्रो वा युगसप्तमे ।
पर्येयन्तश्छुभसंयुक्ता यावत्संख्याग्रहैर्युताः ॥ ८ ॥

Stanza 8.—If the 2nd and the 7th are occupied
by either the lords of the 2nd and the 7th or Venus
and if the 2nd and the 7th are conjoined with or
aspected by benefics, then the number of such
benefics.

तावज्जीवकळत्राणि क्रूरयुक्तास्तुते यदि ।
कळत्रं भगमाप्नोति न्यैकभार्यां विशिष्यते ॥ ९ ॥

Stanza 9.—Indicates the number of living wives
the native will have, while only one wife will live if
malefics join the above combination.

NOTES

The above two stanzas are not difficult but are only con-
fusing. Stanzas 8 and 9 comprehend the following combinations :—

(a) If the lord of the 2nd is in the 2nd and is aspected by or combined with benefics.

(b) If the lord of the 7th is in the 7th and is aspected by or combined with benefics.

(c) If Venus is in the 2nd or the 7th and aspected by or combined with benefics.

(d) If lords of the 2nd and the 7th are in the 2nd and the 7th respectively and are aspected by or combined with benefics, then the number of living wives will correspond to the number of benefics in conjunction with or aspecting the above combinations. If however the planets aspecting the above combinations are malefics instead of benefics, then the native will have only one wife. This may mean that he may have only one surviving wife.

सप्तमस्थो यदि भृगुस्सौरिणा संयुतो यदि ।
स्वस्त्रीसक्क इति प्रोक्तो जातो ज्योतिषकोत्तमैः ॥ १० ॥

Stanza 10.—Astrologers say that if Venus is in the 7th with Saturn, the person will remain attached to his own wife.

सप्तमस्थो यदि बुधः परस्त्रीसक्त उच्यते ।
सप्तमस्थो यदि गुरुः भार्या पतिपरायणा ॥ ११ ॥

Stanza 11.—Mercury in the 7th makes the person addicted to other women. Jupiter in the 7th renders the wife deeply devoted to him.

सप्तमेश कुटुंबेश कर्मेशास्तु चतुर्थगाः ।
परस्त्रीषु रतो जातः इत्यूचुर्गणिका बुधाः ॥ १२ ॥

Stanza   12.—Astrologers say that if the lords of
the 7th, the 2nd and the 10th are in the 4th, the
person will be addicted to other women.

सप्तमस्थः सैंहिकेयः जातेन निपुणो भवेत् ।
सप्तमस्थो यदि ध्वजः भार्यां धूर्थेति कथ्यते ॥ १३ ॥

Stanza   13.—The person becomes skilful if Rahu
is in the 7th. Ketu in a similar situation makes the
wife a shrew.

NOTES

It is very difficult to define exactly the term 'morality'.
Moral values depend upon so many factors. In India, one is
guilty of a moral lapse if he sexually unites with a woman
other than his legal wife. In the West such a lapse is perhaps
normally ignored.

The presence of Mercury in the 7th and the conjunction
of the 2nd, 7th and 10th lords in the 2nd are not conducive
to make the person confine his sexual pleasures to his own
wife.

Thus ends the Sixth Chapter entitled "Seventh House
Indications" in *Bhavartha Ratnakara* of Sri Ramanujacharya.

CHAPTER VII

अथ आयुरारोग्य तरङ्गः

HEALTH AND LONGEVITY

संपश्शरीरसुलाणां कारकस्य गुरोर्यदि ।
लग्नाधिपतिना योगोह्लायुः प्रबलमादिशेत् ॥ १ ॥

Stanza 1.—Jupiter is the indicator (karaka) of
fortune, children and body. Good longevity is indicated if he is combined with the lord of the Ascendant.

आयुष्करेण शनिनाह्यष्टमाधिपतेर्यदि ।
संबन्धो विद्यते यस्य दीर्घायुर्योग उच्चते ॥ २ ॥

Stanza 2.—Long life will be conferred if Saturn
is in conjunction with (or aspected by) the 8th lord.

अष्टमस्थे शनौ जातो दीर्घायुर्योगमाप्नुयात् ।
अष्टमेशे लग्नकेतु अल्पायुष्यं विनिर्दिशेत् । ३ ॥

Stanza 3.—Long life is indicated if Saturn is in
the 8th. The 8th lord in the Ascendant combined
with Ketu confers short life.

NOTES

The author dispenses with the question of longevity
rather briefly. His observations are short, concise and full of

meaning. The importance of the Ascendant – indicating body, and the 8th indicating longevity—is recognised.

Jupiter is said to be the karaka of 'sharira' or body. Several noted writers have opined that the Sun is the *Thanukaraka* or indicator of body. Irrespective of the fact that Jupiter is or is not the karaka of the body, his association with lord of the Ascendant assures good longevity. The span of human life can be brought under four important divisions, viz., *Balarishta or* infant mortality (death before 8 years), *Alpayu* or short life (between 8 and 32 years), *Madhyayu* or middle life (death between 33 and 75) and *Poornayu* or full life (from 75 to 120). For fuller information on the subject I would refer the readers to my *Hindu Predictive Astrology* and *How to Judge a Horoscope*.

Saturn is the *Ayushkaraka* or indicator of longevity and if he is situated in the 8th house, good longevity is assured. The position of the 8th lord in the Ascendant is not at all conducive for long life.

पितृकारक भानोस्तु भाग्याधिपतिना यदि ।
संबन्धो विद्यते यस्य दीर्घायुः पितुरुच्यते ॥ ४ ॥

Stanza 4.—The person's father will be long-lived if the Sun is combined with the lord of the 9th.

भाग्यस्थो यदि भानुस्यादल्पायुष्यं पितुस्तथा ।
चतुर्थे यदि चन्द्रस्तु मातुस्यादल्पजीवितम् ॥ ५ ॥

Stanza 5.—The father of the person will be short-lived if the Sun is in the 9th. The mother will be short-lived if the Moon is in the 4th house.

भाग्यस्थौ भानुभाग्येशौ आयुर्हीनो भवेत्पिता ।
लाभस्थो यदि भाग्येशौ दीर्घायुर्योगवान् पिता ॥ ६ ॥

Stanza 6.—The native's father will be short-lived
if the Sun and the 9th lord are in the 9th. If however
the lord of the 9th is in the 11th, the father will live
long.

NOTES

Stanzas 4, 5 and 6 give combinations for predicting
father's longevity. These three stanzas make also clear that a
karaka in his respective Bhava destroys the indications of the
said Bhava. Thus the Sun as *Pitrukaraka* (indicator of father)
in the 9th house causes father's death early. However if the
Pitrukaraka (Sun) is combined with lord of the 9th, the father
lives long. It should be noted that this combination should not

Chart No. 35.—*Born on 16–10–1918 at 2–26 p.m.
(I.S.T.), Lat. 13° N. ; Long. 77° 35′ E.*

		Ketu	Jupit.		Saturn Jupiter	
Moon		RASI HJH-12		Rahu	NAVAMSA	Venus
Ascdt.			Sat.	Moon		Ketu
	Mars Rahu	Merc. Sun	Venus	Mars	Merc. Sun	Ascdt.

Balance of Rahu's Dasa at birth : years 11–8–20.

occur in the 9th house. However the 9th lord in the 11th promotes the longevity of the father.

These principles have to be applied very carefully as otherwise the reader is bound to go wrong. In all cases where the Sun is placed in the 9th house, early death to father cannot and should not be predicted. As a matter of fact this is only one of the four factors, *viz.,* the 9th, 9th lord, the *karaka* and the planets placed in the 9th.

In Chart No. 35 the Sun is no doubt in the 9th house, but early death to father cannot be predicted, because the 9th lord is in the 10th having obtained Parivarthana—and is aspected by Jupiter. In Chart No. 36 however the situation of the Sun in the 9th is harmful to father's long life, because the 9th lord Jupiter is in the 8th with Mercury lord of the 3rd and aspected by Saturn.

चतुर्थस्थानपतिना संबन्धो यदि विद्यते ।
मातृकारक चन्द्रस्य मालायुष्यं विनिर्दिशेत् ॥ ७ ॥

Stanza 7.—If the Moon is combined with the lord of the 4th, the mother will have long life.

NOTES

Compare this to stanza 4. The combination of the 4th lord and the Moon is good so far as mother's longevity is concerned but the Moon should not occupy the 4th. The Moon's situation in the 4th is decidedly harmful if he is with Saturn also. In Chart No. 37 the Moon is in the 4th in conjunction with Saturn. The 4th lord Venus is also not well disposed. Hence the native lost his mother in his second year.

Chart No. 36.—*Born on 13–3–1891 at 2–19 p.m. (L.M.T.), Lat. 13° N. ; Long. 77° 35' E.*

Sun	Moon Mars	Rahu		Mercury	Rahu Venus
Mercury Jupiter	RASI 1-89		Ascdt.	NAVAMSA	Moon Sun Mars
Venus			Sat. (R)	Jupit.	
	Ketu			Ketu	Saturn	Ascdt.

Balance of Ketu's Dasa at birth : years 0–9–26.

तृतीये यदि भौमस्तु आतृस्यादल्पजीवितम् ।
तृतीयस्थो यदि गुरुश्रंबारिष्टं वदंति हि ॥ ८ ॥

Stanza 8.—If Mars is in the 3rd, the brothers will be short-lived. If Jupiter is in the 3rd, evil is caused to brothers.

तृतीयस्थो यदि गुरु स्वक्षेत्रस्यात्तृतीयकम् ।
एक एव च आतास्यज्जातकस्य वदंति हि ॥ ९ ॥

Stanza 9.—If the 3rd happens to be owned and occupied by Jupiter, the native will have only one brother.

Chart No. 37.—*Born on 8-8-1912 at about 7-23 a.m. (L.M.T.), Lat. 13° N. ; Long. 77° 35' E.*

	Saturn Moon			Saturn	Venus	
Rahu						
Ascdt.		Sun	Rahu Sun			
	RASI			NAVAMSA		Moon Mercury Ketu
		Mars Merc. Venus	Ascdt.			
	Jupiter	Ketu		Jupiter	Mars	

Balance of Mars' Dasa at birth : years 6-0-10.

NOTES

In stanza 8, the author uses the term *bhratrusyadalpa- jeevitam* for Mars in the 3rd while the term used for Jupiter's position in the 3rd is *bhratrarishtam vadanti hi*. *Arishta* also means loss or death. But in this particular case, I interpret *arishta* as meaning evil. Thus if Mars is in the 3rd the brothers will be short-lived while Jupiter in the 3rd indicates evil to brothers. In other words brothers will not thrive or prosper well. Stanza 9 requires that in order to have only one brother Jupiter must not only be in the 3rd but the 3rd must be a sign owned by Jupiter. This is possible only in respect of persons born in Libra and Capricorn in which case Jupiter becomes the 3rd lord.

आयुर्हीनं च पुत्रस्य गुरुः पञ्चमगो यदि ।
अल्पायुष्यं कळत्रस्य भृगुस्सप्तमगो यदि ॥ १० ॥

Stanza 10.—Jupiter in the 5th diminishes the longevity of the son. Venus in the 7th makes the wife short-lived.

चतुर्थेशश्चन्द्रमाश्च भाग्ये राज्येऽथ लाभगे ।
पञ्चमेहिस्थितौस्यातां मातुः दीर्घायुषं वदेत् ॥ ११ ॥

Stanza 11.—Predict long life to the native's mother if the 4th lord and the Moon are in the 9th, the 10th, or the 5th.

चतुर्थेशः चतुर्थस्यः मूलकोणं भवेद्हितम् ।
दीर्घमायुस्समाप्नोति मातेत्यूचुर्बुधोत्तमाः ॥ १२ ॥

Stanza 12.—The learned in astrology say that if the 4th lord is in the 4th and it happens to be Moolatrikona for the 4th lord, then the mother will be long-lived.

चतुर्थेशश्च चन्द्रश्च प्रबलस्थान संस्थितौ ।
क्षीणी चन्द्रो यदि भवेच्चतुर्थेशनिवीक्षितं ।
अल्पायुष्यं समाप्नोति जातस्य जननी ध्रुवम् ॥ १३ ॥

Stanza 13.—If the 4th lord and waning Moon are in the 4th aspected by Saturn, the native's mother will be short-lived.

NOTES

Stanza 10 only confirms the common dictum that a *karaka* in his respective Bhava destroys the indications of the Bhava concerned. Jupiter in the 5th makes the son short-lived, Venus in the 7th makes the wife short-lived. With due defference to the great author of this work I have to submit that my own personal experience (which is not meagre) warrants that I should respectfully disagree with the common notion that Jupiter in the 5th and Venus in the 7th are bad for those two Bhavas. If Jupiter is in the 5th, the native will not only have a son as the first issue but he will live long. Similarly Venus in the 7th makes the wife beautiful, fair and passionate. If Jupiter and (or) Venus are afflicted by Mars, the native will not derive much happiness from the sons and the wife. If Rahu or Saturn be the afflicting body, then you can predict short life to the sons or wife.

Stanzas 11, 12 and 13 are only an extension of the principle adumbrated in stanza 5, wherein it is stated that the Moon in the 4th is not conducive to the life of the mother. Under certain special circumstances the evil nature of the combination referred to in stanza 5 will be cancelled and these exceptions are dealt in stanzas 11 and 12.

Thus ends the Seventh Chapter entitled "Health and Longevity" in *Bhavartha Ratnakara* of Sri Ramanujacharya.

CHAPTER VIII

अथ भाग्ययोग तरङ्गः

FORTUNATE COMBINATIONS

भाग्यमाधिपो लाभगे वा लाभेशो भाग्यगो यदि ।
लाभ भाग्याधिपत्येश्व संबन्धे भाग्यमादिशेत् ॥ १ ॥

Stanza 1.—If the lord of the 9th is in the 11th and the lord of the 11th is in the 9th or if the 9th and 11th lords are conjoined together or aspect each other, the native will be fortunate.

द्वन्द्वीभूयग्रहश्राष्टौ वेद संख्यासु राशिषु ।
स्थिताश्चेद्बहुभाग्यस्तु वक्तव्यो जातकस्य हि ॥ २ ॥

Stanza 2.—The native will be fortunate if eight planets occupy four houses in pairs of two each.

द्वन्द्वीभूयग्रहाष्टा च गुणसंख्यासु राशिषु ।
स्थिताश्चेद्भाग्ययोगस्तु वक्तव्यो जातकस्य हि ॥ ३ ॥

Stanza 3.—The person will be fortunate if six planets occupy three signs in pairs of two each.

चतुर्णां शुभ खेटानां पापखेटक वीक्षणम् ।
नास्ति चेद्भाग्य बाहुल्यं धनयोगं समश्नुते ॥ ४ ॥

Stanza 4.—If four benefics are aspected by malefics, the person will not be very fortunate but he will have some wealth.

तृतीय षष्ठ लाभेषु स्थिताश्चेत् क्रूर खेचारा: ।
जातस्य योगो भाग्यस्य वक्तव्यस्सूरिभिस्तथा ॥ ५ ॥

Stanza 5.—The person becomes fortunate if malefics occupy the 3rd, 6th and 11th houses.

यद्भावकारको लग्नाद्द्व्यये तिष्ठति चेद्यदि ।
तस्य भावस्य सर्वस्य भाग्ययोग उदीरित: ॥ ६ ॥

Stanza 6.—The person will be fortunate in respect of that Bhava whose karaka is situated in the 12th from the Ascendant.

NOTES

Bhagya implies fortune as different from wealth. A man may command any amount of wealth but still he cannot be called fortunate if he is devoid of children, if his relations are inimically disposed, if his wife is quarrelsome and if his reputation and name are sullied. Thus 'fortune' is an invisible goddess whom no wealth can court. In this chapter, the author refers to the various combinations which make a man generally 'fortunate'. According to stanza 2, a person will be very fortunate if the eight planets are situated in four houses in pairs of two each. This combination more or less corresponds to *Kendra Yoga*—one of the 7 Sankhya Yogas referred to in

Brihat Jataka, with this difference that our author specifies the number of planets as 8, which includes Rahu also, while the author of *Brihat Jataka* has ignored Rahu in his treatment of Sankhya Yogas. The planets must occupy four houses in pairs of two each. Here again the reader should use his intelligence in differentiating the results. If the four signs happen to be the 7th to 10th houses, then the native's fortune will be generally centered on the indications of these houses while if the four houses are 10th to 1st, the degree of fortune and the source from which it flows must necessarily differ.

Stanza 4 is important because it gives a combination, which while making one wealthy, renders him unfortunate. The four benefics are the waxing Moon, well associated Mercury, Jupiter and Venus. These should be free from malefic aspects.

In Chart No. 38 it will be seen that all the four benefics are subjected in some way or other to malefic aspects—the exception being that the Moon is waxing and that Saturn though a malefic is lord of the Ascendant. The original clearly says 'papakheta veekshanam' meaning 'should be aspected by malefics'. Here no reference is made to the question of association and conjunction. Therefore if we accept the combination literally, then it means that the native will not be fortunate if the four benefics are aspected by malefics and that if there is association with malefics, the evil stands greatly minimised. This combination in its modified form applies to the above horoscope. Jupiter is aspected by Saturn while the Moon, Mercury and Venus are not aspected. Thus the native is fortunate in regard to children, wife, name, fame, profession and money matters.

Stanza 5 says that in Upachayas (3, 6 and 11) malefics promote fortune.

Chart No. 38.— *Born on 8-8-1912 at about 7-23 p.m. (L.M.T.), Lat. 13° N.; Long. 77° 35' E.*

Rahu	Saturn Moon		Saturn	Venus
Ascdt.	**RASI**	Sun	Rahu Sun	
		Mars Merc. Venus	**NAVAMSA** Ascdt.	Moon Mercury Ketu
Jupiter		Ketu	Jupiter	Mars

Balance of Mars' Dasa at birth : years 6-0-10.

Stanza 6 gives an important clue. It says that the native will be fortunate only in respect of such Bhavas whose karakas are in the 12th from the Ascendant. Here emphasis is laid on the *karaka of the Bhava* and not on the lord of the Bhava. The following are the important karakas for the different Bhavas :—

Thanubhava	or	1st house	The Sun
Dhanabhava	,,	2nd ,,	Jupiter
Bhratrubhava	,,	3rd ,,	Mars
Matrubhava	,,	4th ,,	The Moon
Putrabhava	,,	5th ,,	Jupiter
Satrubhava	,,	6th ,,	Saturn
Kalatrabhava	,,	7th ,,	Venus
Ayurbhava	,,	8th ,,	Saturn
Pitrubhava	,,	9th ,,	The Sun

Karmabhava	or 10th house	Jupiter
Labhabhava	,, 11th ,,	Jupiter
Vyayabhava	,, 12th ,,	Saturn

Thus if the Sun is in the 12th from the Ascendant, the native will be fortunate in respect of 9th house indications; if the Moon is in the 12th, in respect of 4th house indications; if Venus is in the 12th, in respect of the 7th house indications and so on.

Chart No. 39 :—*Born on 12–2–1856 at 12–21 p.m. (L.M.T.), Lat. 18° N. ; Long. 84° E.*

	Moon Rahu	Ascdt.	Sat.	Jupit.		Ascdt.	Rahu
Sun Mercury Jupiter		RASI				NAVAMSA	
		III–85		Merc.			
Venus		Mars Ketu		Ketu		Moon, Sun Saturn Venus Mars	

Balance of Venus' Dasa at birth :   years 6–11–3.

In Chart No. 39 the Moon karaka for the 4th house is in the 12th from the Ascendant and hence the native was fortunate in respect of mother.

But note the Moon is with Rahu aspected by Mars. The mother died in the 12th or 13th year.

वाहनेशश्च शुक्रश्च सप्तमेश्वर भाग्यपौ ।
लाभभाग्यगतौस्तेस्तु शानि संबन्धिनो यदि ॥ ७ ॥

Stanza 7.—If the lord of the 4th, Venus, lord of the 7th and lord of the 9th are in the 11th or the 9th and are aspected by or conjoined with Saturn,

तद्दशान्तर्देशाकाले गजवाहन लाभकृत् ।
बृहज्जातक योगोयं सूरिमिः परिकीर्तितः ॥ ८ ॥

Stanza 8.—The native will have access to elephants in the course of the period and sub-period of Saturn. This yoga is ascribed to *Brihat Jataka* by the learned in astrology.

NOTES

In the modern times very few people can think of possessing elephants and riding on them excepting a few religious heads. However the Yoga may be taken to mean that one would have access to conveyances either in Saturn's Dasa or in Saturn's Bhukti provided (*a*) the lord of the 4th is in the 9th or the 11th in conjunction with or aspected by Saturn, (*b*) Venus is in the 9th or 11th in conjunction with or aspected by Saturn, (*c*) the lord of the 7th occupies the 9th or the 11th in conjunction with or aspected by Saturn and (*d*) the lord of the 9th is in the 9th or the 11th aspected by or combined with Saturn.

लग्नभाग्य चतुर्थेशाः राज्येशेन च राज्यगाः ।
अथवा लग्नदारस्थाः तेषां दायेथवान्तरे ॥ ९ ॥

Stanza 9.—If the lords of the Ascendant, the 9th and the 4th are in the 10th, the 1st or the 7th in conjunction with the lord of the 10th, then during the periods and sub-periods of such lords,

काले सिंहासनप्राप्ति लभते बहुभाग्यभाक् ।
महत्कीर्तिं समायुक्तो भवतीत्यनु शुश्रुमः ॥ १० ॥

Stanza 10.—The native will ascend the throne, becomes very fortunate and enjoys wide fame.

NOTES

This is one of the important *Maharaja Yogas* and is a rare one too. One becomes a king, enjoying fame and prosperity in the course of the Dasa or Bhukti of the lords of the Ascendant, the 9th and the 4th if such lords are combined with the 10th lord—all occupying the 10th house or the Ascendant or the 7th.

पञ्चमे भाग्यराशौ वा उच्चस्था खेचरा स्थिताः ।
जातो योगमवाप्नोति कीर्तिंचापि समश्नुते ॥ ११ ॥

Stanza 11.—If an exalted planet is situated in the 5th or the 9th, the person becomes fortunate and famous.

सूर्यं शुक्र बुधाः पुत्रे लाभस्थश्च भवेद्गुरुः ।
बुधदाये विशेषेण धनभाग्यं समश्नुते ॥ १२ ॥

Stanza 12.—The native earns much wealth in the course of Mercury Dasa if the Sun, Venus and Mercury are in the 5th and Jupiter is in the 11th.

पितृकारक भावोश्च भाग्यभावेश्वरोपि वा ।
उभौ तौ व्ययगौस्यातां पितृभाग्यमुदीरितम् ॥ १३ ॥

Stanza 13.—Predict fortune through father if both the Sun and the lord of the 9th are together in the 12th house.

सूर्यमेषं गतेचैव पितृभाग्यमुदीरितम् ।
तुलायां यदि वा भानुः भाग्यहीनो भवेदिपता ॥ १४ ॥

Stanza 14.—The native's father will be fortunate if the Sun is exalted. The father will be unfortunate if the Sun is debilitated.

धनुर्लग्ने तु जातस्य पितृभाग्यमुदीरितम् ।
तुलायां संस्थितोपिस्याद्विस्तलैव भाग्यदः ॥ १५ ॥

Stanza 15.—Predict fortune through father for a person born while Sagittarius is rising. Even if the Sun is in Libra free flow of fortune will not be obstructed.

व्ययेश भाग्यराशीश्च सूर्याणां संस्थितिव्यंये ।
पितृस्तु भाग्ययोगश्च व्यये देवेज्य रिःफपौ ॥ १६ ॥

Stanza 16.—The native's father will be fortunate if the lords of the 12th, the 9th and the Sun are in the 12th, or if Jupiter and lord of the 12th are in the 12th.

NOTES

Ordinary *Dhana Yogas* are mentioned in stanzas 11 and 12. They are simple to understand and easy to apply, and hence call for no explanation. Stanza 13 is more or less a repetition of the idea given in stanza 6. The native will be fortunate in respect of father, and he will be happy, if the Sun is exalted ; the reverse holds good if the Sun is debilitated. This principle does not apply in case of Sagittarius Ascendant — as here the Sun will be lord of the 9th and situated in the 11th causing a favourable Yoga. Somehow the author seems to lay special emphasis on the fact that a Bhava shines well if the appropriate karaka is in the 12th from the Ascendant. This statement of the author should be accepted with due reservation.

Let us take the Moon. He is the karaka for the 4th house. If he is the 12th from the Ascendant it means he is in the 9th from 4th Bhava. Similarly if we take Venus—karaka of 7th house, he will be in the 6th from 7th—if he is situated in the 12th from the Ascendant. The 6th is an Upachaya. If we take Mars—Karaka of the 3rd, he will be in the 10th—if he is placed in the 12th from the Ascendant. A karaka in particularly good position from the appropriate Bhava renders the Bhava beneficial. The author must have had this idea when he formulated the general principle referred to in the above stanzas.

व्यये शुक्रस्य संस्थानं कळत्राद्भाग्यमुदिशेत् ।
व्यये चन्द्रस्य संस्थानं मातृभाग्यमुदिरितम् ॥ १७ ॥

Stanza 17.—The native will be fortunate in respect of wife and mother respectively if Venus and the Moon are in the 12th from the Ascendant.

कुजो व्यये स्थितो यस्य भ्रातृभाग्यमुदीरितम् ।
भाग्येशः कुत्रलं रिःफे पितृभाग्यमुदीरितम् ॥ १८ ॥

Stanza 18.—Whoever has Mars in the 12th will be fortunate in respect of brother. If the 9th lord is in the 12th, the native will be fortunate in regard to father.

भाग्याधिपस्सप्तमस्थः भाग्ये सप्तसनायकः ।
कळल भाग्यमाप्नोति स्वार्जितं धनमेव च ॥ १९ ॥

Stanza 19.—If the 9th lord is in the 7th and the 7th lord is in the 9th, the person will be fortunate in regard to wife, and he will have self-earned wealth.

द्वितीयेशा बुधष्षष्ठे ज्ञातीनां धनमश्नुते ।
केवल तु बुधष्षष्ठे ज्ञातीनां धनमश्नुते ॥ २० ॥

Stanza 20.—The native acquires money through cousins if the 6th is occupied by Mercury and the 2nd lord. If Mercury alone is in the 6th, then also he will get money through cousins.

पञ्चमेशोपि वागीशो उच्चस्थानस्थितो यदि ।
भाग्यवन्तस्तस्य पुत्रा इति ज्योतिषकोविदुः ॥ २१ ॥

Stanza 21.—The learned in astrology opine that one's children will become fortunate if Jupiter, as lord of the 5th, is exalted.

NOTES

The chapter is headed by *Bhagya Yoga* or Fortunate Combinations. In other words these combinations help us to decipher as to how one could be happy and fortunate in regard to wife, brothers, cousins, parents and the like. They also reveal how gain of money is shown through different relatives. The combination mentioned in stanza 21 holds good only with reference to person born in Leo and Scorpio Ascendants.

Thus ends the Eighth Chapter entitled "Fortunate Combinations" in BHAVARTHA RATNAKARA of Sri Ramanujacharya.

CHAPTER IX

अथ राजयोगतरङ्गः

RAJA YOGAS

द्वितीय पञ्चमेशौ तु द्वितीये पञ्चमे यदि ।
भाग्यराज्ये स्थितौ वापि राजयोगप्रदौ श्रुतौ ॥ १ ॥

Stanza 1.—Raja Yoga is caused if the 2nd and 5th lords are in the 2nd and 5th houses or in the 9th and 10th houses respectively.

धनलाभाधिपौ राज्ये दोषादि रहितौ स्थितौ ।
तयोर्दाये तु संप्राप्ते राजयोगप्रदौ इह्तौ ॥ २ ॥

Stanza 2.—If the 2nd and 11th lords are in the 10th free from debilitation, inimical conjunction, combustion and other evil dispositions, then Raja Yoga will be conferred on the native in the course of the Dasas of such lords.

राज्यलाभचतुर्थेषु पञ्चमे वा स्थितो यदि ।
राजयोगप्रदो राहुस्तद्दशान्तर्दशासु च ॥ ३ ॥

Stanza   3.—Rahu gives rise to Raja Yoga in his own Dasa and Bhukti if he occupies the 10th, 11th, 4th or 5th house.

केतोस्तृतीय संस्थानं योगदं भवति ध्रुवम् ।

भाग्यापत्यस्थ केतुस्तु न शुभो दोषमावहेत् ॥ ४ ॥

Stanza   4.—Ketu in the 3rd will certainly give rise to yoga.   If he is in the 9th or the 5th, he be- comes inauspicious and causes evil.

तृतीये चन्द्रशुक्रौ तु स्थितेचेद्योगदो भृगुः ।

शुक्रदाये तु संप्राप्ते शुक्राद्योगं समश्नुते ॥ ५ ॥

Stanza   5.—Venus becomes a yogakaraka if the Moon and Venus are in the 3rd.   During Venus Dasa fame will be conferred.

राज्याधिपस्तृतीये च लाभे वा यदी संस्थितः ।

सर्वत्र योगोना भवेत्कुलचिच्च भविष्यति ॥ ६ ॥

Stanza   6.—If the 10th lord is in the 3rd or the 11th, no permanent yoga is given rise to. There will be slight yoga at some time.

राज्याधिपोपि च गुरुस्तृतीये यदि संस्थितः ।

आतृशत्रु यथा योगः कथयोगप्रदो गुरुः ॥ ७ ॥

Stanza   7.—If Jupiter happening to be lord of the 10th is in the 3rd, he will give rise to the same yoga that he would do, were he lord of the 3rd.

NOTES

Raja Yoga means a combination indicating political power, fame and prosperity. It is very difficult to define the word *Raja Yoga*. Yoga in Sanskrit means a combination or configuration of planets and Raja Yoga implies special combination denoting political power and fame. Raja Yogas are many and have several gradations. A village magistrate, a tribal chief, a monied man, an influential landlord, a petty king, an independent prince and a great emperor have all Rajayogas as also the president of a republic and the manager of a large manufactory. Thus Raja Yoga means exercise of some power—political, religious, administrative, magisterial or executive. To get real political power the Sun, the Moon and Mars must be powerful. Political power is different from power of learning, of money, personal influence and indescribable tact. We see often in our experience men without money, without Government service, without landed properties wielding a power over their fellow-subjects, quite inexplicable. His power is not based on any temporal advantages. Readers must look to the sources of strength and weakness of the planets causing the *Raja Yoga* and then prescribe the rank. Raja Yoga may be taken to mean power and fame.

The combinations given in this chapter are indeed full of significance. As the stanzas are simple, they do not require any further elucidation.

In Chart No. 40 note there is a conjunction of the 2nd and 11th lords, *viz*, Mercury and Jupiter in the 10th, free from affliction. This has given rise to a powerful Raja Yoga (*vide* Stanza 2). My book How To Judge A Horoscope deals with Raja Yogas rather exhaustively and the reader may refer to it for fuller explanations. The principles contained in the above

stanzas may be summed up as follows for the information of
the reader.

Chart No. 40:—*Born on 12–2–1856 at 12–21 p.m.*
(L.M.T.), Lat. 18° N ; Long. 84° E.

	Moon Rahu	Ascdt.	Sat.	Jupit.		Ascdt.	Rahu
Sun Mercury Jupiter		RASI				NAVAMSA	
Venus		Mars Ketu		Ketu		Moon, Sun Saturn Venus Mars	

Balance of Venus' Dasa at birth :   years 6–11–3.

1.   Lords of the 2nd and the 5th should be in the 2nd and
the 5th or in the 9th and the 10th to cause Raja Yoga.

2.   The 2nd and 11th lords should be in the 10th free
from affliction.

3.   Rahu should be in the 10th, the 11th, the 4th or the
5th to confer Raja Yoga in his Dasa.

4.   Ketu's presence in the 3rd is good, but inauspicious in
the 9th and the 5th.

5.   Venus becomes capable of conferring power if he is in
the 3rd with the Moon.

6.   The native does not always wield power if the 10th
lord is in the 3rd or the 11th but will do so only temporarily.

Illustrative of some of the combinations given above are
the following chart (Chart No. 41) :—

Chart No. 41 : *Born on 10–9–1889 at about sunrise.*
Lat. 13° N. ; Long. 77° 35' E.

			Rahu	Rahu	Mars	Saturn	Jupiter
Moon							
			Venus				Mercury Moon
	RASI				NAVAMSA		
	HJH-53		Mars Sun Sat. Ascdt.				
Ketu Jupiter			Merc.	Venus	Sun Ascdt.		Ketu

Balance of Jupiter's Dasa at birth :   years 1–1–13.

In Chart No. 41 it will be seen that lord of the 2nd Mercury is in the 2nd and that of the 5th is in the 5th. This has no doubt given rise to Raja Yoga especially because Mercury the 2nd lord is exalted. But Jupiter's association with Ketu going under the technical name of *Guruchandala Yoga* has somewhat marred the Raja Yoga.

Chart No. 41 given above illustrates the Raja Yoga mentioned in stanza 1. In Chart No. 42 given herewith Jupiter is lord of the 2nd and the 11th and he is in the 10th. This is a very auspicious combination in as much as finance, gains and means of livelihood are brought together so that all these three functions are promoted. Jupiter Dasa in the case of the native of Chart No. 42 has produced very beneficial results in respect of money, fame, profession and gains.

Chart No. 42 :—*Born on 8–8–1912 at about 7–23 p.m. (L.M T.) Lat. 13° N. ; Long. 77° 35' E.*

Rahu	Saturn Moon			Saturn	Venus	
Ascdt.	RASI III-54	Sun	Sun Rahu	NAVAMSA		Moon Mercury Ketu
		Mars Merc. Venus	Ascdt.			
	Jupiter	Ketu		Jupiter	Mars	

Balance of Mars' Dasa at birth :   years 6–0–10.

Chart No. 43 :—*Born on 7–5–1861 at 4–2 a.m. (L.M.T.) Lat. 22° 40' N. ; Long. 88° 30' E.*

Ascdt. Moon	Sun Mercury Venus	Mars Ketu	Jupit. Ascdt.		Ketu	Mercury
		Jupit.		NAVAMSA		Saturn
	RASI 4-83	Sat.	Moon			
Rahu				Venus Sun Rahu	Mars	

Balance of Mercury's Dasa at birth :   years 9–5–22.

This horoscope (Chart No. 43) illustrates the principle adumbrated in stanza 3 that Rahu in the 10th house confers Raja Yoga in his Dasa. Rahu by himself is not capable of giving rise to any results. He gives the effects of the lord of Rasi which he occupies. Consequently, in this particular chart Rahu must cause the result of Jupiter who as lord of the Ascendant and the 10th lord is exalted in the 5th. This is a unique combination which has made the subject a great figure in the field of poetry and literature.

According to stanza 6, if the 10th lord is in the 3rd, the native does not always enjoy Raja Yoga but will do so only temporarily. In this horoscope (Chart No. 44) the 10th lord Venus is in the 3rd in his own house with Mercury lord of finance. The native was once very well off and commanded much influence but now he is humble. Mark the Dwirdwadasa position of planets.

Chart No. 44:—*Born on 29-9-1888 at 4-35 a.m. (L.M.T.) Lat. 26° 30' N ; Long. 74° 45' E.*

		Moon		Sun	Moon
		Sat. Rahu	Sat. Ketu	**NAVAMSA**	
RASI			—		
Ketu		Ascdt.	Mars		Rahu
	Mars Jupiter	Mercury Venus	Sun	Merc. Ascdt Venus	Jupiter

Balance of Jupiter's Dasa at birth : years 5–5–23.

Stanza 7 is rather vague. It says that if Jupiter as 10th lord (which is possible in case of Gemini and Pisces Ascendants) is in the 3rd, he would give rise to the same Yoga as he would do, if he were lord of the 3rd. What results Jupiter would give as lord of the 3rd the author has not elucidated. We have to take the information from other books.

भाग्याधिपश्चाष्टमस्थस्तद्दाये नैवयोगद: ।

भाग्याधिपोपि च गुरोर्ह्यष्टमस्थोपि भायगद् ॥ ८ ॥

Stanza 8.—If the 9th lord is in the 8th, his Dasa will not confer any fame. If Jupiter as lord of the 9th is in the 8th, the person becomes highly fortunate.

NOTES

This is an important stanza not only as enunciating a general principle but as pointing out an exception. Thus the 9th lord in the 8th is not good. But Jupiter is an exception. In our humble experience we have found that if Jupiter, even without being lord of the 9th, is in the 8th the native enjoys much wealth. But such Jupiter should be lord of the Ascendant. The horoscope (Chart No. 45) illustrates this principle.

The Ascendant is Sagittarius and the lord Jupiter is exalted in the 8th. There are of course several other good combinations but this one has made the native amsas much fortune.

रध्रंभाग्याधिपल्योश्च संबन्धो यदि विद्यते ।

अष्टमाधिपतेर्द्दाये संप्राप्ते योगमादिशेत् ॥ ९ ॥

Stanza 9.—If the 8th and 9th lords are in conjunction or aspect each other, fame and power will be conferred in the Dasa of the 8th lord.

Chart No. 45:—*Born on 31–1–1896 at 4–40 a.m. (L.M.T.) Lat. 22° 20′ N ; Long. 73° E.*

			Moon		Sun Saturn
Mercury Rahu	RASI	Moon Jupit.	Rahu	NAVAMSA	Venus
Sun	III–112	Ketu			Ketu Mars
Ascdt. Mars Venus	Saturn		Mercury	Jupiter	Ascdt.

Balance of Mercury's Dasa at birth :   years 2–3–1.

NOTES

This combination is to be found in Chart No. 45. The Sun and the Moon lords of the 9th and the 8th respectively aspect each other so that the Moon's Dasa will confer fame and prosperity on the native.

भाग्यरन्ध्राधिपत्योश्च संबन्धो यदि विद्यते ।
भाग्येशदाये संप्राप्ते नैवयोगप्रदोह्मसौ ।
अष्टमाधिपतेरंतर्दशायां योगदो भवेत् ॥ १० ॥

Stanza 10·—If the 9th and 8th lords combine with or aspect each other, fame and power will be conferred not in the Dasa of the 9th lord but in the sub-period of the 8th lord.

NOTES

In stanza 9, it is stated that the 8th lord gets the power to produce Yoga which means the 9th lord delegates his power to the 8th lord with the result he himself becomes powerless.

राज्यलाभाधिपत्योश्च संबन्धो यदि विद्यते ।
लाभाधिप दशाकाले राजयोगो भविष्यति ॥ ११ ॥

Stanza   11.—If the 10th and 11th lords combine with or aspect each other, Raja Yoga will be caused in the Dasa of the 11th lord.

राज्यलाभाधिपत्योश्च संबन्धो यदि विद्यते ।
गर्येशदाये संप्राप्ते समयोग उदीरितः ॥ १२ ॥

Stanza   12.—If the 10th and 11th lords combine with or aspect each other, good and bad results will be equal during the Dasa of the 10th lord.

लाभेशान्तर्दशाकाले योगहीनो भवेत् ध्रुवम् ।
दशमस्थ भृगोः पाके न योगं लभते नरः ।
सप्तमस्थः शनेः पाके राजयोगं समश्नुते ॥ १३ ॥

Stanza   13.—The person will be deprived of fame and prosperity in the sub-period of the 11th lord. When Venus is in the 10th no Yoga will be produced in his Dasa. Raja Yoga will be conferred in Saturn Dasa if Saturn is in the 7th house.

NOTES

In Chart No. 46 note lord of the 10th aspects the lord of the 11th while from Chandra Lagna lord of the 10th and the 11th aspect each other mutually. The native has been enjoying

Chart No. 46 :—*Born on 8-8-1912 at about 7-23 p.m. (L M.T.) Lat. 13° N. ; Long. 77° 35' E.*

Rahu		Saturn Moon			Saturn	Venus	
Ascdt.	**RASI**		Sun	Sun Rahu	**NAVAMSA**		
			Mars Merc Venus	Ascdt.			Moon Mercury Ketu
Jupiter		Ketu			Jupiter	Mars	

Balance of Mars' Dasa at birtn :   years 6-0-10.

Raja Yoga in the Dasa of Jupiter, lord of the 11th (stanza 11). The principle given out in stanza 13 that the sub-period of the lord of the 11th would deprive the native of Raja Yoga is applicable *in toto* to the above example.   In the sub-period of Jupiter (in the Dasa of Jupiter) the native lost fame and money and his reputation was at stake for no fault of his.   There was a clear break in the Raja Yoga.

सप्तमस्थस्तैर्हिकेयो योगदो भवति ध्रुवम् ।
तृतीय भाग्यगो मन्दो योगप्रद इति स्तृतः ॥ १४ ॥

Stanza 14.—Rahu in the 7th will certainly confer fame and prosperity.   Saturn in the 3rd and the 9th will also confer Yoga.

तृतीयाष्टम भाग्यस्थो गुरुर्गोगप्रदो भवेत् ।
द्वादशस्थो यदि गुरुर्देवलोकं समश्नुते ॥ १५ ॥

Stanza 15.—Jupiter in the 3rd, the 8th and the 9th will confer fame and prosperity. The person goes to heaven after death if Jupiter is in the 12th.

भाग्यराज्याधिपौ राज्ये भाग्ये वा यदि संस्थितौ ।
राजयोगमवाप्नोति महतीं कीर्तिमश्नुते ॥ १६ ॥

Stanza 16.—If the 9th and 10th lords are in the 10th and the 9th respectively, the native will enjoy Raja Yoga and much fame.

NOTES

The Yogas mentioned in stanzas 14 and 15 are simple enough. Contrary to the commonly accepted notion that Saturn destroys the Bhava he occupies, the author holds that Saturn in the 9th confers Yoga. But readers will have to note that such a situation of Saturn would adversely affect the father. The 12th represents *moksha* or emancipation. As Jupiter is a Deva planet his situation in the 12th takes the person to heaven after his death.

The combination given in stanza 16 goes under the name of *Dharmakarmadhipa Yoga* or exchange of houses between 9th and 10th lords and it is an auspicious combination. Though it may not give much fame, it will certainly confer prosperity and wealth.

In Chart No. 47 lord of the 9th Mercury is in the 10th while the 10th lord Venus is in the 9th. Though Venus is debilitated, he is free from Neecha effect. The native is very well off in life and enjoys much prosperity.

Chart No. 47:– *Born on 16–10–1918 at 2–26 p.m. (I.S.T) Lat. 13° N. ; Long. 77° 35' E.*

		Ketu	Jupit		Saturn Jupiter	
Moon	RASI HJH-12		Rahu	NAVAMSA		Venus
Ascdt.			Sat.	Moon		Ketu
	Mars Rahu	Sun Mercury	Venus	Mars	Mercury Sun	Ascdt.

Balance of Rahu's Dasa at birth :   years 11–8–20.

राज्यस्था यदि भाग्येशः राज्येशो भाग्यगो यदि ।
राजयोगमवाप्नोति महतीं कीर्तीमश्नुते ॥ १७ ॥

Stanza 17.—If the 9th lord is in the 10th and the 10th lord is in the 9th, the native enjoys much fame and power.

NOTES

This is merely a repetition of stanza 16 in a different form and is quite unnecessary.

भाग्यधिपो भाग्यगतो राज्येशो राज्यगो यदि ।
राजयोगमवाप्नोति महतीं कीर्तीमश्नुते ॥ १८ ॥

Stanza 18.—The person enjoys much fame and power if the 9th lord is in the 9th and the 10th lord is in the 10th.

राज्येश पञ्चमेशौ तु राज्ये वा पञ्चमेथवा ।

स्थितौ चेद्योगमाप्नोति महतीं कीर्तिमश्नुते ॥ १९ ॥

Stanza 19.—Power and fame are conferred if the 10th and 5th lords are in the 10th and the 5th.

भाग्यराज्याधिपौ यत्र सप्तमस्थौ च लग्नगौ ।

राजयोगमवाप्नोति महतीं कीर्तिमश्नुते ॥ २० ॥

Stanza 20.—Power and fame are conferred if the 9th and 10th lords are in the 7th and 1st houses respectively.

रिपुसप्तम राज्येशाः केन्द्रस्था यदि कोणगाः ।

राजयोगं च लभते महतीं कीर्तिमाप्नुयात् ॥ २१ ॥

Stanza 21.—If the 5th, 7th and 10th lords are situated in quadrants or trines, the person enjoys power and much fame.

मेषे रवि कर्कटस्थौ जीवचन्द्रौ तुला शनि ।

मकरस्थो भवेद्भौमौ राजयोग उदीरितः ॥ २२ ॥

Stanza 22.—Raja Yoga is caused if the Sun is in Aries, Jupiter and the Moon are in Cancer, Saturn is in Libra and Mars is in Capricorn.

NOTES

Stanzas 18 to 20 inclusive suggest the combinations which confer Raja Yoga. Such combinations are to be found in almost all horoscopes of any pretence to power. The 10th, the 9th, the 5th, the 7th and the 1st houses are taken into account and certain dispositions of these lords are said to confer Raja Yoga.

It is not clear as to why the 6th lord is given importance along with the 7th and 10th lords in stanza 21. Probably the 6th lord will lose the evil of 6th lordship if he is in a kendra or trikona but still the evil will be there and it will manifest in some shape in the period or sub-period of the 6th lord.

	Sun		
			Moon Jupiter
	Chart No. 48 III-58		
Mars			
	Saturn		

The combination given in the last stanza is to be found in very rare and exceptional cases as for instance in the horoscope of Sri Rama.

The Moon and Jupiter are in Cancer. The Sun is in Aries, Saturn is in Libra and Mars is in Capricorn thus causing a very powerful Raja Yoga. The same combination will be found in the horoscopes of several well-known Emperors of Puranic fame.

CHAPTER X

अथ गंगादिपुण्यस्नान योगः

COMBINATIONS FOR DIPS IN SACRED WATERS

कर्मकारक देवेन्द्र पूज्यस्य यदि विद्यते ।
संबन्ध कर्मनाथेन त्वत्कर्मनिरतो भवेत् ॥ १ ॥

Stanza 1.—If Jupiter is combined with or aspected by the lord of the 10th, the native will be engaged in good deeds.

कलपुत्रभाग्येशाः गुरुकर्माधिपतौ तथाः ।
जलराशि स्थिता सर्वेद्यान्योन्यसंगता यदि ॥ २ ॥

Stanza 2.—If the lords of the 7th, the 5th, the 9th, Jupiter and the 10th or all combined in an aquatic sign (Jalarasi).

गुरुदाये च संप्राप्ते गंगातुल्यनदीषु च ।
स्नानसिद्धिर्भवेत्सेव गंगास्नानं न सिद्ध्यति ॥ ३ ॥

Stanza 3.—The native will have dips in rivers as sacred as Ganga but in Ganga in the course of Jupiter Dasa.

पुखदारेशदायेतु यात्राकार्यं न सिद्ध्यति ।
पुण्यइलोकस्य विण्णोश्च कथासु निरतो भवेत् ॥ ४ ॥

Stanza 4.—No pilgrimage will be undertaken in the Dasas of the 5th and the 7th lords. The native will devote himself to listening to the stories of Vishnu.

युग्मजातस्य भाग्यस्थौ गुरुमन्दौ तयोर्देशा ।
काले भवति गगायाः स्नानं भवति निश्चयः ॥ ५ ॥

Stanza 5.—A person born in Gemini Ascendant will certainly have dips in Ganga in the Dasas of Jupiter and Saturn if they are in the 9th house.

मेषलग्ने तु जातस्य शुक्रेज्यार्यम्णो यदि ।
राज्यस्थास्तद्दशाकाले गंगास्नानं भविष्यति ॥ ६ ॥

Stanza 6.—A person born in Aries Ascendant will bathe in Ganga in the Dasas of Venus, Jupiter and the Sun if they are in the 10th house.

कर्मांधिपो गुरुयुतः कर्मप्राबल्यमादिशेत् ।
षष्ठव्ययस्थः कर्मेशः कर्महीनो भवेन्नरः ॥ ७ ॥

Stanza 7.—If the 10th lord is combined with Jupiter, the native will be highly religious or orthodox. If the 10th lord is in the 6th or the 12th, he will not be religious.

NOTES

That a separate chapter should have been devoted to giving combinations for bathing in sacred rivers shows the importance which the Hindus have attached from time immemorial to the question of pilgrimage. Careful study reveals that pilgrimage to which a religious touch was given was undertaken as part of education. Pilgrimage is the final phase of education and it has its own moral, intellectual and social values. The waters of Ganga and several other sacred rivers are full of medicinal virtue and a dip in these rivers is held so sacred that it washes not only the physical dirt but the mental impurity also. Even now the majority of the Hindus or for that matter people of all religions yearn to undertake pilgrimages so that their existence on the earth might be justified.

Chart No. 49 : – *Born on 8–8–1912 at about 7–23 p.m. (L.M.T.) Lat. 13° N. ; Long. 77° 35' E.*

Rahu		Saturn Moon				Sat.	Venus
Ascdt.	**RASI** III-54		Sun	Rahu Sun	**NAVAMSA**		
			Mars Merc. Venus	Ascdt.			Moon Mercury Ketu
	Jupiter		Ketu		Jupiter	Mars	

Balance of Mars' Dasa at birth :   years 5–6–15.

The first stanza says that if the 10th lord and Jupiter are conjoined together or aspect each other the native will be engaged in *Satkarmas* or good deeds. Jupiter is the Guru or preceptor of the Gods and as the 10th is the house of action. Jupiter's connection with it or its lord is bound to have very

favourable influences.   Human nature takes different moulds.
There are people who are always for destruction, wicked acts,
selfishness and engaged in dirty and scandalous things. Jupiter
in the 10th generally counteracts this evil influence and makes
the native fear God and hate injuring others, detest evil company
and engage himself in charitable acts and deeds.

In Chart No. 49, Jupiter—the *Karmakaraka*—is in the 10th.
In Jupiter s Dasa in his own Bhukti the native had dips in not
only the Ganga but also in other sacred rivers and visited a
number of holy places.

Thus ends the Tenth Chapter entitled "Rajayogas" in
BHAVARTHA RATNAKARA of Sri Ramanujacharya.

CHAPTER XI

अथ मारकतरङ्गः

COMBINATIONS FOR DEATH

व्ययेशस्य दशाकाले धनेशो मारको भवेत् ।
द्वितीयेश दशाकाले व्ययेशो मारको भवेत् ॥ १ ॥

Stanza 1.—The 2nd lord becomes maraka in the Dasa of the 12th lord. The 12th lord becomes a maraka in the Dasa of the 2nd lord.

व्ययनाथ दशाकाले द्वितीयेशेन संगताः ।
द्वितीयेशेन दृष्टाश्च मारकप्रबलइरुताः ॥ २ ॥

Stanza 2.—If the 12th lord is aspected by or is in conjunction with the 2nd lord, he becomes a powerful maraka in his Dasa.

न्दितीयेश दशाकाले व्ययस्थानस्थिताः खगाः ।
व्ययाधिपतिना दृष्टाः प्रबला मारकइरुताः ॥ ३ ॥

Stanza 3.—The planets in the 12th house which are aspected by the 12th lord become powerful maraka during the Dasa of the 2nd lord.

NOTES

Maraka or death is an important event in the life of an individual. I have dealt with this question fairly exhaustively in my books HINDU PREDICTIVE ASTROLOGY and HOW TO JUDGE A HOROSCOPE. The ancient seers have given a number of methods —mathematical as well as predictive—for finding the duration of life of an individual. As far as my humble experience goes, the mathematical methods have their own pitfalls and do not seem to yield correct results in the majority of cases. The predictive processes on the other hand, if handled properly by an expert who has developed intuition, will be very helpful in finding the time of death.

Whatever be the combinations given for finding the maraka planets one should first ascertain whether a horoscope in question indicates *Balarishta* (early death). *Alpayu* (short life), *Madhyayu* (middle life) or *Purnayu* (full life). Generally speaking if the majority of the planets are disposed in Kendras or quadrants, one will have long life : if in *Panaparas* (cadent houses) middle life ; and if in *Apoklimas* (succeedant houses) short life. This is only a general principle and it should be applied with great care. There are well-known principles which will enable any reader of average intelligence to judge the kind of Ayurdaya, and they can be studied from any standard book.

The author of this work, Sri Ramanuja, has given beautiful combinations. According to him:—

(*a*) The 2nd lord becomes a maraka in the Dasa of the 12th lord and *vice versa*. This means that death will be caused in the sub-period of the 2nd lord if the 12th lord happens to be a maraka. Similarly death will be caused in the

sub-period of the 12th lord if the 2nd lord happens to be a
maraka. The 12th or 2nd lord may become marakas by virtue
of association with or being aspected by the 7th or 2nd lords.
I have been a little round about in my explanation because
stanza 1 says that the 2nd lord becomes maraka in the Dasa of
the 12th lord. How can the 2nd lord cause maraka unless as
sub-lord in the Dasa of the 12th lord? This clearly means that
the 12th lord must also become a maraka.

(*b*) The 12th lord becomes a powerful maraka in his Dasa
if he is associated with or aspected by the 2nd lord.

(*c*) Maraka can take place in the sub-periods of the
planets occupying the 12th and who are aspected by the 12th
lord within the Dasa of the 2nd lord.

व्ययनाथ दशाकाले तत्तस्थाः पापिनाः खगाः ।
तेषां अन्तर्दशाकाले मारकस्तु भवन्ति ते ॥ ४ ॥

Stanza 4.—Death may take place in the sub-
periods of malefics occupying the 12th within the Dasa
of the 12th lord.

न्दितीयराशिस्थितपापखेटा दशाविपाके व्ययनाथ संगताः ।
तन्भुक्तिकाले च त एव पापिनो ग्रहस्तथा मारक-
                                         नायकस्युः ॥ ५ ॥

Stanza 5.—Malefic planets who are in the 2nd
house in conjunction with the 12th lord will cause
death in their own Dasa and Bhukti.

व्ययराशिस्थ पापिनां दशाकाले तु मारकः ।
द्वितीयाधिप संबन्धी सचराः पापिनो ग्रहाः ॥ ६ ॥

Stanza 6.—Death will be caused in the Dasa periods of malefics placed in the 12th house. Planets in association with the 2nd lord will also become evil.

NOTES

Stanzas 3 to 6 inclusive are an extension of the principles given in the 1st three stanzas, with slight variations, suggesting the circumstances under which 12th and 2nd lords become marakas. The author seems to be inclined to the view that the 12th lord gets empowered to kill, by his association with the 2nd lord or (evil) planets in the 2nd house. Obviously it means that good planets in the 2nd house even if they are aspected by or associated with the 12th lord cannot become marakas (unless of course they get death-inflicting power otherwise)

अष्टमेश दशाकाले तर्भुक्तौ सोऽपि मारकः ।
षष्ठेशदाये निधनं रन्ध्रेशान्तर्हुतो भवेत् ॥ ७ ॥

Stanza 7.—Death will be caused by the 8th lord in his own Dasa and Bhukti. Death will also be caused in the sub-period of the 8th lord within the Dasa of the 6th lord.

अष्टमेश दशाकाले षष्ठराशिस्थ पापिनाम् ।
हृतौ जातस्य निधनं वदन्ति विबुधोत्तमाः ॥ ८ ॥

Stanza 8.—Astrologers opine that death will be caused by malefics in the 6th, in their sub-periods.

षष्ठनाथ दशाकाले अष्टमस्थ खगस्य च ।
हृतौ जातस्य निधनं वदन्ति विबुधोत्तमाः ॥ ९ ॥

Stanza 9.—Astrologers predict death to the native in the Dasa of the 6th lord and sub-period of the 8th lord.

अष्टमेश दशाकाले अष्टमेशेन वीक्षिताः ।

षष्ठेश संगता ये च तान्वदन्ति हि मारकान् ॥ १० ॥

Stanza 10.—Planets who are aspected by the 8th lord and planets who are associated with the 6th lord become marakas in the Dasa of the 8th lord.

अष्टमास्थितपापस्य दशाकाले वदंति हि ।

षष्ठस्थानपतेरन्तर्दशाकालो हि मारकः ॥ ११ ॥

Stanza 11.—Death will be caused in the Dasa of a malefic occupying the 8th and the sub-period of the 6th lord.

षष्ठस्थितस्य पापस्य दशाकाले वदंति हि ।

अष्टमाधिपतेरन्तर्दशाकाले हि मारकः ॥ १२ ॥

Stanza 12.—Death will happen in the Dasa of a malefic occupying the 6th house and the sub-period of the 8th lord.

षष्ठस्थितस्य पापस्य दशाकाले वदन्ति हि ।

अष्टमस्थितस्य रन्ध्रेश भुक्तिकालो हि मारकः ॥ १३ ॥

Stanza 13.—Death will occur in the Dasa of a malefic occupying the 6th, and in the sub-period of the 8th lord placed in the 8th house.

अष्टमस्थित पापस्य दशाकाले वदंति हि ।

षष्ठस्थितस्य पापस्य मुक्तिकालो हि मारकः ॥ १४ ॥

Stanza 14.—Death will happen in the Dasa of a malefic occupying the 8th and in the Bhukti of a malefic posited in the 6th.

NOTES

Stanzas 7 to 14 inclusive describe combinations which cause death by certain dispositions of the 6th and 8th lords. The 6th is the house of disease and the 8th is the house of life or Ayus. In all the above principles, no reference is made to the 7th lord. For the information of the reader I may just enunciate the general principles governing maraka. The author of this work has given some importance to the lords of the 8th and the 6th. But in the general principles, the 6th and 8th lords become of tertiary importance because death is to be predicted in their Dasas, provided the Dasas of other planets declared as marakas are not likely to operate. Prof. B. Suryanarain Rao's English Translation of JATAKA CHANDRIKA make these principles very clear.

(1) Lord of the 2nd or the 7th is a maraka.

(2) Malefic occupants of these two houses.

(3) Malefic planets in association with these lords.

(4) Benefics in association with the 2nd and 7th lords.

(5) Lords of the 7th and the 8th.

(6) Lord of the 3rd or the 8th associated with the 2nd or 7th lord.

(7) Saturn in association with a maraka.

(8) Lord of the 6th or 8th whether or not he is associated with a maraka.

(9) The least powerful planet in the horoscope.

According to this author, death may occur in the Dasas and Bhuktis of the following planets which we are tabulating herewith for the information of the reader.

Dasa or Period	Bhukti or sub-period
(1) Lord of the 8th.	Lord of the 8th.
(2) Lord of the 6th.	Lord of the 8th.
(3) Lord of the 8th.	Malefic in the 6th.
(4) Lord of the 6th.	Planet in the 8th.
(5) Lord of the 8th.	Planets in association with the 6th lord; planets aspected by the 8th lord.
(6) A malefic occupant of the 8th.	The 6th lord.
(7) A malefic occupant of the 6th.	The 8th lord.
(8) A malefic occupant of the 6th.	8th lord occupying the 8th.
(9) A malefic occupant of the 8th.	A malefic occupant of the 6th.

बुधशुक्रौ पञ्चमस्थांविन्योन्यौ मारकौ स्मृतौ ।
बुधदाये तु शुक्रस्तु शुक्रदाये बुधस्तथा ॥ १५ ॥

Stanza 15.— If Mercury and Venus are in the 5th house, they become mutual marakas.

NOTES

If Mercury and Venus are together in the 5th, then death may occur in the Bhukti of Mercury within the Dasa of Venus and *vice versa*. The combination is vague and it naturally implies that when these two planets are in the 5th and if according to the usual rules of maraka determination Mercury becomes a maraka in his Dasa, then Venus will cause death in his Bhukti ; if Venus becomes a maraka in his Dasa, Venus kills the native in his Bhukti.

कूराधिपत्य शुक्रस्तु कुज: पञ्चमगो यदि ।
कुजदाये तु संप्राप्ते करोति निधनं कुज: ॥ १६ ॥

Stanza 16.—Mars causes death in his own Dasa if he has evil lordship and is placed in the 5th house.

NOTES

Evil lordship means owning the 6th, the 8th and the 12th houses. This can happen only when the Ascendant is Aries, Taurus, Virgo, Scorpio and Sagittarius. Mars should not only wn either the 6th, the 8th or the 12th house but should also be placed in the 5th to cause death in his Dasa.

अधिकाराराष्छुमो मन्दो मारकग्रह संयुत: ।
अतीव बलवान्गृत्स्यो मारक प्रबलस्स्मृत: ॥ १७ ॥

Stanza 17.—Even though Saturn may own favourable houses, he becomes powerful in causing death by being in conjunction with other marakas.

NOTES

Saturn is Ayushkaraka and the power to kill devolves on him if he joins death-inflicting planets. The good influences contributed by his favourable ownership cannot minimise Saturn's power to cause death. Saturn becomes favourable by virtue of owning a Kendra or an angle, and by owning both a Kendra and Thrikona together which is possible in case of Taurus and Libra Ascendants.

लग्नस्थ रन्ध्रनाथस्य दशाकाले तु मारक: ।
रन्ध्रेषा एव भवतीत्याहुरुज्जीतक कोविद: ॥ १८ ॥

Stanza   18.—Astrologers opine that death will be caused in the Dasa of the lord of the 8th who occupies the Ascendant.

द्वेरूयाणां पुत्राणां संप्राप्ते राहुदायके ।
पितुर्नोधनमित्याहुस्तद्द्शामध्य एव च ॥ १९ ॥

Stanza   19.—If two or three sons of the native undergo Rahu Dasa simultaneously, then the person will die in his Dasa. And he will enjoy ordinary results.

NOTES

Stanza 18 is clear and requires no explanation. According to stanza 19, death of the person will happen in Rahu Dasa of his 2 or 3 sons—if they are to enjoy the said period simultaneously.

Thus ends the eleventh chapter entitled ''Combinations for Death'' in BHAVARTHA RATNAKARA of Sri Ramanujacharya.

अथ महादशाफल तरङ्गः

RESULTS OF DASAS

शुक्रान्तरे शनेर्दायें शुक्रदायें तथा शने ।
अन्तर्दशायां संप्राप्ते योगहीनो भवेन्नरः ॥ १ ॥

Stanza 1.—The person becomes unfortunate during Saturn's Dasa Venus Bhukti or Venus Dasa Saturn's Bhukti.

शनिर्दायें तु शुक्रस्तु शुक्रदायें शनिस्तथा ।
मीने धनुषि जातस्य योगदो भवति ध्रुवम् ॥ २ ॥

Stanza 2.—For persons born in Sagittarius and Pisces Acendants, Venus and Saturn give rise to Yoga in the Dasas of Saturn and Venus respectively.

NOTES

As we have already said elsewhere, *Yoga* means affluence and fortunate results in general. One becomes devoid of affluence in Saturn's sub-period in the major period of Venus and in the sub-period of Venus within the Dasa of Saturn. This cannot be accepted a rule or principle. There are several exceptions. Why should Saturn always produce evil results in the Dasa of Venus and *vice versa* ? In actual practice instances

have come to our notice wherein Venus has produced affluence
and riches in the Dasa of Saturn and *vice versa*. The following
horoscope will illustrate our point.

Chart No. 50 :— *Born on 7–8–1887 at 1–30 p.m. (L.M T.)
Lat. 11° N. ; Long. 77° 22' E.*

		Mars	Rahu		Mars	
Moon		Sun Merc. Rahu Sat.	Sun Venus			Moon
	RASI			NAVAMSA		
Ketu	HJH–53					
	Ascdt.	Jupiter	Venus	Jupit.	Ascdt.	Mercury	Ketu Saturn

Balance of Jupiter's Dasa at birth : years 0–7–6.

In this horoscope Ascendant is Scorpio.   Saturn is lord of
the 3rd and the 4th and occupies the 9th while Venus as lord
of the 7th and the 12th occupies the 11th. Saturn and Venus
are disposed in the 3rd and the 11th from each other. In the
Navamsa the situation of Venus is favourable. Hence this sub-
period of Saturn in the major period of Venus did not cause
any harm to the native. On the other hand, he enjoyed the
sub-period with beneficial results. Though stanza 1 says that
the sub-period of Venus in the Dasa of Saturn and that of
Saturn in the Dasa of Venus would produce injurious results
due consideration must be shown to the general strength of
these two planets in a horoscope.

The combination given in stanza 2 is however an exception to the one suggested in stanza 1 in as much as the principle that Saturn and Venus give rise to evil results in the Dasa of Venus and Saturn respectively should not be applied to persons born in Pisces and Sagittarius Ascendants. For Pisces Ascendant, Saturn owns the 11th and 12th houses and Venus rules over the 3rd and the 8th. Thus both are malefics and probably on account of similar disposition in reference to Pisces Ascendant their evil dispositions may get counteracted and they be enabled to give rise to favourable results.

षष्ठाष्टमव्ययस्थ रन्ध्रेशास्य द्वितियंदा ।

षष्ठाष्टमव्ययेशानां भुक्तिकाले हि मारकः ॥ ३ ॥

Stanza 3.—Death may be caused by the lords of the 6th, 8th and 12th houses in the course of the Dasa of the 8th lord who occupies the 6th, the 8th or the 12th.

राज्यविक्रमपत्योश्च संबन्धो यदि विद्यते ।

राज्येशदाये च योगस्तुयोगो विक्रमेशतुः ॥ ४ ॥

Stanza 4.—If the lords of the 10th and the 3rd are in conjunction with, or aspect each other, the native will be deprived of fortune in the Dasa of the 10th lord and he will enjoy fortunate results in the Dasa of the 3rd lord.

NOTES

The 3rd lordship is bad for any planet whereas a benefic owning the 10th becomes a temporary malefic while a malefic owning the 10th becomes a temporary benefic. When the 3rd and the 10th lords join together, then the 3rd lord gets the power to bestow fortunate results.

अपत्य भार्ये भाग्येशाः निजराशिषु संस्थिताः ।
तद्दशान्तर्दशा प्राप्ते गंगास्नान समश्नुते ॥ ५ ॥

Stanza 5.—If the 5th, the 7th and the 9th lords are in their own houses, they give rise to dips in Ganga during their periods and sub-periods.

सप्तमस्थ विलग्नस्थ दाये स्वार्जित भाग्यभाक् ।
दारास्त भाग्यराशीशदाये स्वार्जित भाग्यभाक् ॥ ६ ॥

Stanza 6.—A person gets wealth by his own exertions in the Dasa of a planet occupying the Ascendant or the 7th house. He will also acquire much wealth by his own efforts in the Dasa of the 9th lord occupying the 7th house.

NOTES

There is a lot of difference between inheriting ancestral wealth and property and acquiring the same by dint of his own efforts. There are periods when in spite of our best efforts we cannot acquire any wealth. One's exertions in the matter of getting wealth will meet with success (a) in the Dasa of a planet occupying the 7th house, (b) in the Dasa of a planet placed in the Ascendant and (c) in the Dasa of the 9th lord who occupies the 7th house.

राहुर्दशायां संप्राप्ते राहुकेतोस्तथा शनेः ।
रवेरन्तर्भुक्तिकाले पिता मरणमाप्नुयात् ॥ ७ ॥

Stanza   7.—The native's father will die in the sub-period of Rahu, Ketu, Saturn or the Sun within the Dasa of Rahu.

केतुर्दशायां संप्राप्ता पितुर्निरणमुच्यते ।
भौममन्दरवीणां च राहोरन्तर्दशासु च ॥ ८ ॥

Stanza   8.—Father's death may be predicted in the sub-period of Mars, Saturn, the Sun or Rahu in the Dasa of Ketu.

धरासूनुर्दशाकाले पितुर्निधनमुच्यते ।
राहुकेतुशनीनां च रवेरन्तर्दशासु हि ॥ ९ ॥

Stanza   9.—Father's death will happen in the sub-periods of Rahu, Ketu, Saturn or the Sun in the Dasa of Mars.

शनेर्मेहर्दशाकाले पितुर्निधनमुच्यते ।
राहुभौमरवीणां च केतोरन्तर्दशासु हि ॥ १० ॥

Stanza   10.—Father will die in the sub-period of Rahu, Mars, the Sun or Ketu in the Dasa of Saturn.

राहोर्मेहर्दशालालात्पूर्वेन्तु निधनं पितुः ।
धरासूनुर्दशाच्छिद्रकाले भवति निश्रयः ॥ ११ ॥

Stanza   11—Father's death will certainly happen just before the end of Mars' Dasa and the beginning of Rahu Dasa.

क्रूरग्रहदर्दशाकाले राहोरन्तर्दशा यदा ।
नथैव निधनं व्रूयुः पितुर्जातक कोविदाः ॥ १२ ॥

Stanza 12.—Astrologers say that one's father will die in the sub-period of Rahu in the Dasa of a malefic planet.

NOTES

Stanzas 7 to 12 inclusive deal with the periods which cause death to father. It will be seen that the various combinations mentioned in the above stanzas do not take into account the ownership of a planet but only their natural or Naisargika classification of malefics. Thus father's death is to happen in the sub-period of any malefic planet within the major period of any malefic.

The ending of a Dasa goes under the technical name of *Dasachchidra* and it is generally supposed to produce evil results. According to stanza 11, death of father will happen just before the ending of Mars' Dasa and the beginning of Rahu Dasa. This may be taken to mean that in Mars' Dasa when the sub-period of a malefic is current, *viz.,* Ketu or the Sun, the father may die.

गुरुशुक्रौ वृश्चिकस्थौ शुक्रदाये समागमे ।
राजयोगकरश्शुक्रो भवेदेव न संशयः ॥ १३ ॥

Stanza 13.—Venus confers Raja Yoga in his Dasa if he is in conjunction with Jupiter in Scorpio.

रवेस्सोमसुतस्यापि संबन्धे यदि विद्यते ।
बुधदाये प्रबलदो रवे दायस्थु मध्यमः ॥ १४ ॥

Stanza 14.—When the Sun and Mercury are in conjunction with or aspect each other highly favourable results will be caused in the Dasa of Mercury while Sun's Dasa will be ordinary.

चन्द्रमंगल संबन्धे चन्द्रदाये बहुप्रद: ।
कुजदाये तु संप्राप्ते कुजदायस्तु मध्यम: ॥ १५ ॥

Stanza 15.—When the Moon and Mars are in conjunction, or aspect each other, fortunate result will be experienced in the Moon's Dasa while the Dasa of Mars will be quite ordinary.

गुरुशन्योश्च संबन्धे शनिदाये विशेषद: ।
गुरुदाये च संप्राप्ते तद्दृशा मध्यमास्मृता ॥ १६ ।

Stanza 16.—When Jupiter and Saturn join together or aspect each other Saturn's Dasa will prove very fortunate while Jupiter's Dasa will be ordinary.

गुरोरङ्गारकन्यापि संबन्धे यदि विद्यते ।
भौमदायास्थूत्तमस्य गुरुदायस्तु मध्यम: ॥ १७ ॥

Stanza 17.—When Jupiter and Mars are in conjunction or aspect each other, Mars' Dasa will be very fortunate and Jupiter's Dasa will be ordinary.

गुरोस्सुधांशु संबन्धे चन्द्रदायो विशेषद: ।
गुरोर्देशा संप्राप्तौ गुरुदायस्तु मध्यम: ॥ १८ ॥

Stanza 18.—When Jupiter and the Moon join together, the Moon's Dasa will prove highly prosperous while Jupiter's Dasa will be ordinary.

NOTES

Stanzas 13 to 18 give interesting combinations to enable us to predict the relative good and bad nature of the results of Dasas of different planets in conjunction or mutual aspect.

These combinations can be summarised as follows for the convenience of our esteemed readers :

Two planets in conjunction or in mutual aspect	Dasa in which highly benefic results will happen	Dasa in which ordinary results will happen
1. Venus and Jupiter in conjunction in Scorpio	Venus	...
2. The Sun and Mercury	Mercury	the Sun
3. The Moon and Mars	the Moon	Mars
4. Jupiter and Saturn	Saturn	Jupiter
5. Jupiter and Mars	Mars	Jupiter
6. Jupiter and the Moon	the Moon	Jupiter

It will be seen from the above that Jupiter is to produce only ordinary results in any of his combinations with Mars, the Moon and Saturn. This is however a general principle and it stands to be modified if Jupiter becomes a yogakaraka or has some special distinction by way of exaltation or situation in the Ascendant, or the 10th or the 2nd or the 11th or the 9th house. The above tabulation will also enable us to anticipate that in the course of the Dasa of the planets which are supposed to give ordinary results, beneficial results will happen within the sub-periods of those whose major periods are supposed to prove highly fortunate. Thus if you take Jupiter and Saturn, then Saturn's Bhukti in Jupiter's Dasa will bet highly fortunate.

In Chart No 51 it will be seen that (a) Jupiter and Saturn aspect each other, (b) Mars aspects Jupiter and (c) Jupiter and the Moon aspect each other. Consequently Saturn's Dasa will be much more beneficial than Jupiter's. The native will no enioy the Dasa of the Moon and Mars. The sub-period of the

Chart No. 51.—*Born on 8–8–1912 at about 7–23 p.m. (L.M.T.), Lat. 13° N., Long. 77° 35' E.*

Rahu	Saturn Moon			Saturn	Venus
Ascdt.	**RASI**	Sun	Sun Rahu	**NAVAMSA**	Moon Mercury Ketu
		Mars Merc. Venus	Ascdt.		
	Jupiter	Ketu		Jupiter	Mars

Balance of Mars' Dasa at birth : years 6–0–10.

Moon, Mars and Saturn will also prove much more beneficial than the sub-periods of other planets in Jupiter's Dasa. Here we have not taken into account the strength or weakness of any of these planets. Jupiter's Dasa, Jupiter's Bhukti proved very unfortunate to the native as Jupiter is in Scorpio in the 10th house, whereas the fortunes were considerably advanced in the Bhukti of Saturn. Saturn is lord of the Ascendant and he is in the 4th in a friendly sign aspected by Jupiter, lord of the 2nd. Moreover for Lunar Ascendant Saturn becomes a Yogakaraka and his situation in Chandra Lagna aspected by Jupiter enables him to give much more favourable and fortunate results than Jupiter.

The combinations of the Moon and Mars, Jupiter and Mars, and Jupiter and the Moon go under the special distinction of *Chandramangala Yoga, Gurumangala Yoga* and *Gaja-*

kesari Yoga respectively and out of the two planets causing
each Yoga, one becomes capable of producing much more
favourable results than the other. It will be seen that only
"ordinary results" will happen in the Dasa of the other planet
and not unfortunate results.

केन्द्रकोणस्य राहोश्च दायकाले समागमे ।
स्वतन्त्र राजयोगं च महत्कीर्ति समश्नुते ॥ १९ ॥

Stanza 19.—Rahu will confer Raja Yoga and
much fame in his Dasa if he joins a quadrant or a trine.

गुरोर्बुधस्य शुक्रस्य संबन्धो यदि विद्यते ।
विशेष धनयोगश्च कीर्तिमान्भाग्यवान् भवेत् ॥ २० ॥

Stanza 20.—If Jupiter, Mercury and Venus join
together or are in mutual aspect, the native becomes
very wealthy, famous and fortunate.

शुक्रस्य यदि संबन्धो बुधेन गुरुणापि वा ।
शुक्रदाये च संप्राप्ते धनयोगं लमेश्वरः ॥ २१ ॥

Stanza 21.—The native will earn much wealth in
Venus' Dasa if Venus is in conjunction with or
aspected by Mercury or Jupiter.

गुरुदाये च संप्राप्ते धनहीनो भवेन्नरः ।
बुधस्यदाये संप्राप्ते मिश्रयोगो भवे ध्रुवम् ॥ २२ ॥

Stanza 22.—The native becomes bereft of wealth
in the Dasa of Jupiter and mixed results will be
produced in the Dasa of Mercury when the said
planets are disposed as per stanza 21.

NOTES

Rahu when occupying a kendra (quadrant) or Trikona (trine) is supposed to give rise to Raja Yoga in his Dasa.

If Jupiter, Mercury and Venus are in mutual conjunction, or aspect, one becomes fortunate and wealthy. All these three planets are benefics (Mercury becomes benefic here as he will be with the other two benefics) but only one of the three in combination can really enable the native to acquire wealth in his Dasa. Stanza 22 makes the meaning very clear. If Venus is in conjunction with or aspected by Mercury or Jupiter, then :

(a) Venus confers wealth in his Dasa.

(b) Jupiter causes loss of wealth in his Dasa and

(c) Mercury produces mixed results in his Dasa.

Remember that for each of these three planets to produce the results ascribed above, they must conjoin together or aspect each other. If Venus and Jupiter make up the combination the latter gives evil results and if Venus and Mercury cause the combination, the latter produces mixed results.

रव्यादि ग्रह्योगसंयोगे रवेदांये समागमे ।

रविर्योगदयित्युक्तः इतरे मध्यमस्तृताः ॥ २३ ॥

Stanza 23.—If the Sun and other planets combine together, the Sun confers fame and wealth in his Dasa while the other planets give ordinary results.

ग्रहे रन्यैश्च राल्होस्तु संबन्धो यदि विद्यते ।

यो ग्रहाः प्रबलस्तेषां तत्फलं च ददाति सः ॥ २४ ॥

Stanza 24.—Of the several planets who are in conjunction with or aspected by Rahu, the strongest one gives the results indicated by it.

राहुसूर्यस्तथामन्दस्त तृतीये यदि संस्थिताः ।
राहोर्देशा विपाकस्तु भाग्य विक्रमयोगदः ॥ २५ ॥

Stanza 25.—When Rahu, the Sun and Saturn are
in the 3rd, Rahu gives rise to courage and fortune in
his Dasa.

राहोर्देशा विपाकेतु विक्रमस्थो बुधोर्यदि ।
धैर्यहीनो भवेज्जात इति चातककोविदाः ॥ २६ ॥

Stanza 26.—Astrologers say that during the Dasa
of Rahu one becomes timid if Mercury is in the 3rd
house.

NOTES

If planets are in conjunction with the Sun, they become
astangata or combust. Combustion occurs when the planets
are very near the Sun. Otherwise it cannot be called combustion. If the Sun and other planets join together, the Sun
confers fame and fortune in his Dasa while ordinary results
will be given by the other planets. Stanza 24 requires some
explanation. For example Jupiter, Venus and Saturn are in
conjunction with Rahu. Of these three let us assume that
Jupiter is the most poverful and he owns the 5th house, and
occupies the 9th house. Then Jupiter alone will be able to
produce in his Dasa results of his indication, *viz.*, children and
fortune. The indications of the other two planets become more
or less defunct. The original stanza says, *Rahostusambandho*—
meaning both conjunction and aspect. Of the several planets
aspecting Rahu, the results indicated by that which is most
powerful will manifest in the course of his Dasa in preference
to the others.

Chart No. 52. – *Born on 8–8–1912 at 7–23 p.m. (L.M.T.), Lat. 13° N. ; Long. 77° 35' E.*

Rahu		Saturn Moon			Saturn	Venus	
Ascdt.			Sun	Sun Rahu			
	RASI		Mars Merc. Venus	Ascdt.	NAVAMSA		Moon Mercury Ketu
	Jupiter		Ketu		Jupiter	Mars	

Balance of Mars' Dasa at birth : years 6–0–10.

In Chart No. 52 Rahu is aspected by Mars and Jupiter. The latter's is more powerful. Therefore the indications of Jupiter—finance, professional prospects and gain—will manifest in the course of Jupiter's Dasa. Rahu, the Sun and Saturn are all first-rate malefics. Still if these three are together in the 3rd, Rahu can cause Yoga in his Dasa.

Thus ends the 11th chapter entitled "Results of Dasas" in BHAVARTHA RATNAKARA of Sri Ramanujacharya.

CHAPTER XII

अथ ग्रहसामान्ययोग तरङ्गः

ORDINARY COMBINATIONS

तत्तद्भावेश्वराः खेटाः तत्तक्कारक संयुताः ।
तस्य भावस्य सर्वस्य प्राबल्यं प्रोश्वते बुधैः ॥ १ ॥

Stanza 1.—The learned in astrology say that all such Bhavas whose lords are in conjunction with the respective karakas become strong.

NOTES

Each Bhava comprehends several significations. If a Bhava is strongly disposed, all its significations will fully manifest. A Bhava gets vitality if its lord joins its karaka. Each Bhava has its own karaka, *viz.*, the Sun is the karaka for Ascendant and the 9th (father) ; the Moon is the karaka of the 4th (mother) ; Mars is the karaka of the 3rd (brothers) ; Jupiter is the karaka of the 2nd (wealth) and 5th (children) ; Venus is the karaka of the 7th (wife or husband) ; Saturn is the karaka of the 8th or longevity. Thus the Ascendant Bhava gains strength if its lord joins the Lagnakaraka, *viz.*, the Sun, similarly the 4th Bhava gains vitality if the 4th lord is with the Moon, the karaka for the 4th house.

तृतीयाष्टमैकादशाधिपतिस्त्वन्तु स दोषकम् ।
सुतभाग्याधिपत्यन्तु खेटानां शुभद भवेत् ॥ २ ॥

Stanza 2.—Lords of the 3rd, the 8th and the 11th produce evil. Lords of the 5th and the 9th give good results.

NOTES

In *Jathakachandrika* which is more or less an epitome of Parasara's work, the ownership of the 3rd, the 6th and the 11th has considered as productive of evil while here, reference has been made to the lordship of the 8th. I have to observe that the 8th lordship is not as malefic as that of the 6th.

तथापि च गुरोराशित्रात् षष्ठाष्टमेशित: ।
रन्ध्रस्थान स्थिताश्रापि योगदा भवति ध्रुवम् ॥ ३ ॥

Stanza 3.—Even Jupiter becomes evil by owning the 3rd, the 6th and the 8th. However, in spite of owning the 8th he will confer fame and wealth.

NOTES

An important principle is enumerated in this stanza. Jupiter becomes a malefic as lord of the 3rd, the 6th or the 8th but his power to confer Yoga will not be obstructed even if he owns the 8th. This means that in his Dasa, he will confer fame, name and wealth but on account of the stigma due to this ownership he may give rise to malefic results as sub-lord in his Dasa or in that of other planets.

शुक्रस्य षष्ठसंस्थानं योगदं भवति ध्रुवम् ।
व्ययस्थितस्या शुक्रस्या यथा योगं वदन्ति हि ॥ ४ ॥

Stanza 4.—Venus in the 6th will certainly give rise to fame and affluence. He will give the same results in 12th house also.

राज्यलाभ चतुर्थेषु पञ्चमे वा स्थितो यदि ।

राहुर्योगप्रदः प्रोक्तो विद्वद्भिर्जातक कोविदैः ॥ ५ ॥

Stanza 5.—Astrologers say that fame and affluence are conferred if Rahu is in the 10th, 11th, 4th and 5th houses.

केन्द्राधिपति यस्सौम्य खेटाय दिनयोगदाः ।

केन्द्रस्था केन्द्रनाथस्तु क्रूरश्चेद्राजयोगदः ॥ ६ ॥

Stanza 6.—Benefics become evil by owning kendras. Malefic planets produce Raja Yoga by owning or occupying kendras.

NOTES

We are coming to the general principles of astrology. Venus becomes beneficial in the 6th and 12th houses. Rahu gives rise to Yoga by occupying the 10th, 11th, 4th and 5th houses. For natural benefics such as Jupiter, Venus and well-associated Mercury lordship of kendras or quadrants is not desirable. Natural malefics, *viz.*, Mars, Saturn, Sun and badly associated Mercury may even cause Raja Yoga by owning or occupying kendras. Prof. B. S. Rao used to tell me that a natural malefic cannot become a Yogakaraka by the mere fact of owning a kendra. At best he will lose his evil nature. The notes given to stanza 6 of *Jataka Chandrika* by Prof. B. S. Rao, in his English translation, are very illuminating and deal exhaustively with the question of malefics and benefics owning kendras.

यस्मिन् भावे स्थितो मन्दो य भावं वीक्षितेथवा ।
तस्य तस्यापि भावस्यन्यूनतां च वदन्ति हि ॥ ७ ॥

Stanza 7.—The house which is occupied or
aspected by Saturn becomes defective.

NOTES

This is a very important combination and is full of significance. Saturn destroys the indications of the Bhava in which
he is situated except the 8th house, If he is in the 2nd, you
will see that the native will never save any money in spite of
big earnings. He will die a pauper or in very adverse financial
circumstances. Of course there are exceptions to this rule
when Saturn is a Yogakaraka. When Saturn is in the 10th
house he will not destroy the indication. On the contrary, he
gives fame, name leadership and the like. But he gives the
subject a sudden fall. The next stanza gives certain exceptions
to the general principle enunciated in stanza 7.

विक्रमं भाग्यराशिश्च शनिना वीक्षितो यदि ।
तस्य भावस्य प्राबल्यमित्यूचुर्गणकोत्तमाः ॥ ८ ॥

Stanza 8.—If Saturn aspects the 3rd and 9th
houses, they will gain strength.

क्षीणचन्द्रो विलग्नस्थो मन्दधीरन्यपोषितः ।
पूर्णचन्द्रो विलग्नस्थो गुणवान् धनवान् भवेत् ॥ ९ ॥

Stanza 9.—Weak (waning) Moon in the Ascendant makes the native dull and dependent. He will
become rich and a man of character if the waxing
Moon is in the Ascendant.

विलग्नस्थौ चन्द्रभौमौ वा मृर्ती भाग्यवान् भवेत् ।
चतुर्थेशयुतो भौमः क्षेत्रवान् भवति ध्रुवम् ॥ १० ॥

Stanza 10.—The native becomes fortunate if the Moon and Mars are either in the Ascendant or in the 8th house. He acquires houses if Mars joins the 4th lord.

NOTES

According to stanza 10, *Chandra-Mangala Yoga* occurring in the Ascendant or in the 8th is good. Mars by himself is not good in the 8th as he will kill the wife (or husband) early in life. But Mars, when he is with the Moon in the 8th, loses his evil nature so that the general fortune of the native is promoted.

Mars is the karaka for lands and the 4th house rules houses and landed properties. When Mars is in conjunction with the

Chart No. 53.—*Born on 8-8-1912 at about 7-23 p.m. (L.M.T.), Lat. 13° N. ; Long. 77° 35' E.*

Rahu		Saturn Moon			Saturn	Venus
Ascdt.			Sun	Sun Rahu		
	RASI				NAVAMSA	Moon Mercury Ketu
			Mars Merc. Venus	Ascdt.		
	Jupiter		Ketu		Jupiter	Mars

Balance of Mars' Dasa at birth : years 6-0-10.

lord of the 4th, the native acquires landed properties and houses.

In Chart No. 53 lord of the 4th is in the 7th with Mars. This is indicative of the subject getting access to house properties. The planet owning, occupying or aspecting the 4th or the planet who is in conjunction with the 4th lord will give house property in his Dasa or Bhukti. In the example horoscope the native purchased a house in Jupiter's Dasa (Jupiter aspecting 4th and occupying the house of Mars) Mercury' Bhukti. Mercury is in conjunction with not only the 4th lord but also Mars

चतुर्थेनाथ देवेज्जौ य चतुर्थे यदि संस्थितौ ।
चतुष्पाद् वृद्धियोगो यमित्याहुर्जातककोविदाः ॥ ११ ॥

Stanza 11.—The person acquires cattle and other domestic animals if Jupiter is in the 4th house with the lord of the 4th.

पापमध्वगता भावास्तथा भावेशकारकाः ।
तद्भाव भवराशीश कारका दुःखदायकाः ॥ १२ ॥

Stanza 12.—Any house or its lord or its karaka, if hemmed in between malefics, will produce evil results.

लाभन्याधिपत्योश्च संबन्धो योगदो भवेत् ।
लाभाधिपस्तृतीये वा व्यये वा योगदा भवेत् ॥ १३ ॥

Stanza 13.—If the lords of the 11th and the 12th join together or aspect each other, they produce good results. And the 11th lord produces good results if he occupies the 3rd or 12th house.

सर्वं राशिषु जातस्य भाग्येशोह्यष्टमे यदि ।

न योगं लभते जात सामान्यो भवति ध्रुवम् ॥ १४ ॥

Stanza 14.—For persons born in any Ascendant, the presence of the lord of the 9th in the 8th does not give rise to any Yoga—but only ordinary results will be produced.

षष्ठस्थो यदि वा चन्द्रो बुद्धिकौशल्यवान् भवेत् ।

द्वितीयस्थो भवेच्चन्द्रः नैल चञ्चलवान् भवेत् ॥ १५ ॥

Stanza 15.—The Moon in the 6th makes the native intelligent. He will be fickle-minded if the Moon is in the 3rd.

समरार्योजराश्रीतिश्शास्त्रे तु कथ्यते ।

मेषमारभ्य तत्संख्याज्ञातव्य विबुधोत्तमैः ॥ १६ ॥

Stanza 16.—Astrologers say that beginning from Aries, the zodiacal signs are odd and even.

NOTES

Three elements make up a Bhava and they are the Bhava (house), Bhavadhipathi (lord of the house) and Bhavakaraka (indicator of the house). These three factors should not be hemmed in between malefics. If all the three factors have malefics on either side then, the vitality of the Bhava will be so weak that it stands self-condemned. If however any one of the factors is subject to the presence of malefics on either side, the prospects of the Bhava in question will be fairly good. If two of the elements are subject to this affliction, the strength of the Bhava would indeed be ordinary.

The combination given in stanza 13 that if the 11th and the 12th lords combine together or aspect each other, is important and it will be found to be applicable in a large majority of cases.

In Chart No. 54, lords of the 11th and the 12th are Jupiter and Saturn respectively. Note they are in mutual aspect and this has given rise to an important Yoga or special combination.

The dictum that the fortunes will be ordinary if the 9th lord is in the 8th (*vide* stanza 14) can hold good provided the 9th Bhava is also weak. Otherwise this combination should be applied very cautiously.

Chart No. 54.—*Born on 8–8–1912 at about 7–23 p.m. (L.M.T.), Lat. 13° N. ; Long. 77° 35' E.*

Rahu	Saturn Moon		Saturn	Venus	
Ascdt.	**RASI**	Sun	Rahu Sun	**NAVAMSA**	
		Mars Merc. Venus	Ascdt.		Moon Mercury Ketu
	Jupiter	Ketu		Jupiter	Mars

Balance of Mars' Dasa at birth : years 6–0–10.

The 16th stanza needs no explanation as it deals with the fundamentals of astrology. Aries is in odd sign. Taurus is even. Gemini is odd, Cancer is even and so on.

Thus ends the 12th chapter entitled "Ordinary Combinations" in BHAVARTHA RATNAKARA of Sri Ramanujacharya.

CHAPTER XIII

अथ ग्रहमालिकयोगाः

GRAHAMALIKA YOGAS

लग्नादिबाणसंख्याक राशि गानवखेचरा ।
स्थिताश्चेत्पञ्च खेटाख्य मालिकायोग उच्यते ॥ १ ॥

Stanza 1.—If all the nine planets occupy the five houses from the Ascendant, Panchagrahamalika Yoga is caused.

NOTES

The chapter is headed *Grahamalika Yoga*. In Sanskrit *Malika* means a garland or a wreath of flowers and *Grahamalika* means a wrath of planets. In standard works on astrology, Malika Yoga is defined as the disposition of the seven planets in the seven houses contiguously. If the planets are disposed from the Ascendant, it is the Lagnamalika Yoga, if they are disposed from the 2nd, it is Dhanamalika and so on. When the seven signs beginning from any particular sign are occupied by the seven planets, a semi-circle is formed and the term *Malika* will more or less be justified.

The author of this work takes into account the nine planets (which obviously include Rahu and Ketu) and the dispositions of the nine planets from the Ascendant within a certain number of signs is said to give rise to the different types of Malika.

Chart No. 55.—*Born on 5-10-1942 at 10-17 p.m. (I.S.T.), Lat. 13° N. ; Long. 77° 35' E.*

	Ascdt. Saturn		Venus		Mars
Ketu		Jupit. Moon	Moon		Jupiter Sun Saturn Rahu
	RASI 3-121			NAVAMSA	
		Rahu	Ketu		
	Mercury	Sun Mars Venus		Mercury	Ascdt.

Balance of Mercury's Dasa at birth : years 4-7-2.

Chart No. 56.—*Born on 28/29-8-1898 at 5-33 a.m. (L.M.T.), Lat. 16° 50' N. : Long. 5h. 3m. E.*

	Mars Ketu			Moon	Ketu	Jupiter
	RASI 3-121				NAVAMSA	Ascdt.
Moon		Sun Ascdt. Merc.				Sun
Rahu	Saturn	Jupit. Venus	Merc.	Rahu Mars Saturn		Venus

Balance of Moon's Dasa at birth : years 9-8-12.

Readers should therefore note that according to our author the malika or garland should commence only from the Ascendant while according to other standard works, the mala can commence from any house. Another important difference is, that according to the general principles of astrology the seven planets should occupy the seven houses beginning from any house whereas this author suggests that the nine planets should be disposed within five to nine houses from the Ascendant.

Stanza 1 says that *Panchagrahamalika Yoga* is caused if all the nine planets occupy the first five houses. This should not be confused with the *Pasayoga* mentioned by Varahamihira when dealing with the 32 Nabhasa Yogas. When all planets occupy *any five signs* Pasayoga is caused. Note the distinction between *any five signs* and *within the first five signs*.

A little reflection will show to the reader that *all the nine planets* can never occupy the first five houses because Ketu is always to be in the 7th from Rahu. Either the combination is impossible or it should mean that eight planets should occupy the five houses from the Ascendant. I am inclined to think that the author must have been aware of this error which is discernible even to an elementary student. Why, having known that nine planets cannot occupy the first five or six houses, he has still mentioned the combination, I cannot explain.

Chart No. 55 is an illustration of the *Panchagrahamalika Yoga*, in as much as all the eight planets are in the first five signs from the Ascendant.

Chart No. 56 illustrates *Pasa Yoga* in as much as all the seven planets are disposed in the five houses.

लग्नमारभ्ये तेषा: ऋतु संख्य सुराशिषु ।
स्थितांश्चेषष्ठ खेटाख्यामालिका योग उच्यते ॥ २ ॥

Stanza 2.—If all the planets occupy six houses from the Ascendant, Shashtagrahamalika Yoga is caused.

NOTES

As I have already pointed out all the nine planets cannot occupy the first six houses—only eight can occupy. It is also clear that all the houses (from 1 to 5, 6, 7, 8 or 9) should be occupied and no one house should be vacant, to cause Malika Yoga.

लग्नमारभ्य शैलाख्य संख्य राशिषु खेचरा: ।
स्थितइश्चेत्सप्तखेटाख्या मालिका योग उच्यते ॥ ३ ॥

Stanza 3.—If all the planets occupy the seven houses from the Ascendant, Sapthagrahamalika Yoga is caused.

लग्नमारभ्यवस्वाख्यराशिस्था खेचार यदि ।
अष्टखेचारमालाख्य योगप्रोक्तस्तु सुरिमि: ॥ ४ ॥

Stanza 4.—If all the planets occupy the eight houses from the Ascendant, Ashtagrahamalika Yoga is caused.

लग्नादारभ्य भागाख्य संख्यराशिषु खेचारा: ।
स्थितांश्चेन्नव खेटाख्या मालिका योग उच्यते ॥ ५ ॥

Stanza 5.—If all the planets occupy the nine houses from the Ascendant, Navagrahamalika Yoga is caused.

केचिद्वदन्ति सूर्यादि ग्रहणो क्रमशस्थितिः ।
मालिका ग्रहयोगो यमिश्रिजातककोविदाः ॥ ६ ॥

Stanza 6.—Some astrologers say that Grahamalika Yoga commences from the Sun.

केचिद्वदन्ति लग्नाधिराशिषु क्रमशो ग्रहः ।
स्थिताश्चेद् ग्रहमालाख्य योगोयमिति कोविदाः ॥ ७ ॥

Stanza 7.—And still others say that Malika Yoga
commences from the Ascendant.

NOTES

I have already explained in the notes given above that the
generality of astrologers maintain that *Malika* can commence
from the Ascendant or any house—but seven houses should be
occupied by the seven planets (excluding of course Rahu and
Ketu). Here we take, rather the author wants us to take, into
account all the nine planets and for the first two Grahamalika
Yogas involving 5 and 6 houses only eight planets can be
taken. Nowhere else it seems to have been said that the
counting must be made from the Sun. Consequently reference
to this suggestion made in stanza 6 may be easily ignored.

षष्ठ सप्ताष्ट नवमि संख्याख्याः ग्रहमालिकाः ।
भवन्ति यस्य जातस्य भाग्ययोगप्रदा स्मृताः ॥ ८ ॥

Stanza 8.—A person born in the Grahamalika
Yoga caused by the presence of planets in 6, 7, 8 or
9 houses from the Ascendant will be fortunate.

पञ्चखेटाख्यमालाऽपि यस्य जातस्य विद्यते ।
भाग्ययोगस्तु वक्तव्यस्तस्य ज्योतिषकोत्तमै ॥ ९ ॥

Stanza 9.—Astrologers say that a person born in the Grahamalika Yoga caused by the presence of planets in the five houses from the Ascendant will also be fortunate.

NOTES

In general, all the five types of *Grahamalika Yogas* caused by the presence of the planets in 5, 6, 7, 8 or 9 houses from the Ascendant are said to make a person born in them fortunate. The term used by the author is *Bhagya Yoga*—which liberally translated means 'fortunate combination'. Before illustrating these Yogas I shall make a passing reference to some of the Nabhasa Yogas and also to the *Malika Yoga* as propounded in other standard astrological works.

I have already referred to *Pasa Yoga* and have given an example for it. Pasa Yoga means that all the seven planets should occupy any five signs and not the *first five houses*. One born in Pasa Yoga is said to be talkative, clever in the acquisition of virtue and wealth and he will have sons.

If all the seven planets are in any 6 signs (in contra-distinction to Bhavas or houses) *Damini Yoga* is caused. This is also one of the *Nabhasa Yogas*. According to our author *Shashtagrahamalika Yoga* is caused if all the planets are in six signs from the 1st house. Damini Yoga also produces favourable results.

Readers must be able to appreciate the difference between *Damini Yoga* (Chart No. 57) and Shashtamalika Yoga (Chart No. 58). In Chart No. 57 it will be seen that all the planets (note Rahu and Ketu excepted) are posited in any *six signs* whereas in Chart No. 58 rhe eight planets are occupying the six signs from the Ascendant.

Chart No. 57.—*Born on 7-6-1898 at 1-35 p.m.* (L.M.T.), Lat. 11° N.; Long. 5h. 8m. E.

	Mars	Sun Mercury	Venus Ketu	Merc. Jupit,		Venus	Ketu Mars
				Moon			
Moon	RASI 3-49				NAVAMSA		Sun
Rahu	Saturn		Jupit. Ascdt.	Rahu Sat.			

Balance of Sun's Dasa at birth : years 2-5-16.

Chart No. 58.—*Born on 7-5-1861 at 4-2 a.m. (L.M.T.),* Lat. 22° 40' N.; Long. 88° 30' E.

Ascdt. Moon	Sun Mercury Venus	Mars Ketu	Jupit. Ascdt.		Ketu	Mercury
			Jupit.			Saturn
RASI		Sat.	Moon	NAVAMSA		
Rahu				Venus Sun Rahu	Mars	

Balance of Mercury's Dasa at birth : years 9-5-22.

Now we come to the next Yoga, *viz.,* *Sapthagrahamalika Yoga* which is supposed to be caused if all the nine planets occupy the *seven signs from the Ascendant.* It has its counterpart (note there is no comparison) in *Vallaki Yoga,* one of the *Nabhasa Yogas.* If all planets occupy *any seven signs* Vallaki is caused. The man, born in Vallaki, will be skilled and likes music and dancing.

In Chart No. 59, it will be seen that the seven planets have occupied seven signs. Combinations given in stanzas 5 and 6 are easy of comprehension and they do not require any further explanation.

Chart No. 59.—*Born on 10-5-1903 at Gh. 27-30 after sunrise, Lat 13° N.; Long. 77° 35' E.*

Ketu	Sun	Mercury	Venus		Jupiter	Saturn Mercury
Jupiter				Moon Mars		Rahu
	RASI				NAVAMSA	
Saturn				Ketu		
		Ascdt. Moon	Rahu Mars		Ascdt. Venus Sun	

Balance of Rahu's Dasa at birth : years 6-7-11.

Satayog Manjari (*vide* English Translation by B. Suryanarain Rao) gives a clear explanation of Malika Yoga as also *Jathaka Parijatha.* When all the seven planets occupy the seven houses from the Ascendant, it is *Lagnamalika,* from the 2nd *Dhanamalika* and so on. Thus 12 different *Malika*

Yogas are formed which I am giving below for the readers' information.

There is one more point, which in its very nature is controversial and which I do not propose to deal with in these pages. And that is, whether in reckoning these Yogas. Bhavas should be considered or the Rasis. According to Varahamihira, Rasi, Kshetra, Griha, Riksha. Bha, Bhavana are all synonymous terms. But in common parlance Rasi means sign and Griha or Bhava means house. Our author uses the specific word Rasi and therefore there seems to be no doubt that in the reckoning of Malika Yoga Rasis are meant and not Bhavas.

For *Sankhya Yoga* the signs are considered whereas houses are taken into account for *Akriti Yogas*. However, I do not want the reader to confuse the issue. I have dealt with this subject in some of my articles in the columns of THE ASTROLOGICAL MAGAZINE and in my latest book THREE HUNDRED IMPORTANT COMBINATIONS.

समाराशिस्थ खेटानां सूलकोणाधिपत्यजम् ।
फलमग्रे तु तदनुचेत्तिराधीशातां फलम् ॥ १० ॥

Stanza 10.—Planets occupying even signs produce results pertaining to their trinal ownership in the beginning ; the results due to the other ownership will be conferred afterwards.

ओजराशिस्थ खेटानामितराधिशतां फलम् ।
ल्वग्रे भवति कोणाधिपत्येजं फलमन्यथा ॥ ११ ॥

Stanza 11.—Planets occupying odd signs produce results pertaining to ownership of Rasi, etc.,

Name of Malika Yoga	Definition	Result
1. Lagnamalika	All planets in the seven houses from Lagna	King, Commander, wealthy
2. Dhanamalika	,, ,, 2nd	Very wealthy, dutiful, resolute, unsympathetic
3. Vikramamalika	,, ,, 3rd	Ruler, rich, sickly, surrounded by brave men
4. Sukhamalika	,, ,, 4th	Charitable, liberal, wealthy
5. Putramalika	,, ,, 5th	Highly religious and famous
6. Satrumalika	,, ,, 6th	Greedy, somewhat poor
7. Kalatramalika	,, ,, 7th	C o v e t e d by women and influential
8. Randhramalika	,, ,, 8th	Poor and henpecked
9. Bhagyamalika	,, ,, 9th	Religious, well-to-do, mighty and good
10. Karmamalika	,, ,, 10th	Respected, virtuous
11. Labhamalika	,, ,, 11th	Skillful and lord of lovely women
12. Vyayamalika	,, ,, 12th	H o n o u r e d, liberal and respected

in the beginning ; the results due to trinal lordship will
be conferred afterwards.

NOTES

Take Saturn in Chart No. 60. He is in an even sign. He
owns the Ascendant and also the 12th.

In his Dasa or in his Bhukti, the results due to his ownership of the Ascendant and the 12th house will be produced,
not in the beginning of the Dasa or Bhukti but afterwards, *i.e.*,
in the middle and concluding parts. Take Venus. He is in an
odd sign. He owns a Kendra (4th) and also a Trikona. The
results due to his Kendra ownership will happen in the begin-
ing of his Dasa (or Bhukti) while the results due to trinal
ownership may be produced afterwards, *i.e.*, in the middle
and last parts.

Chart No. 60.—*Born on 8–8–1912 at about 7–23 p.m
(L.M.T.), Lat. 13° N. ; Long. 77° 35′ E.*

Rahu		Saturn Moon			Saturn	Venus
Ascdt.	RASI		Sun	Sun Rahu	NAVAMSA	
			Mars Merc. Venus	Ascdt.		Moon Mercury Ketu
	Jupiter		Ketu		Jupiter	Mars

Balance of Mars' Dasa at birth : years 6–0–10.

रवेः द्वितीयस्थ खगा शीघ्रदाश्च भवन्ति हि ।

रवेस्तृतीयस्थ खगा समानगतयो भवन् ॥ १२ ॥

Stanza 12.—A planet in the 2nd from the Sun possesses swift motion ; the one in the 3rd from the Sun will have even motion.

रवेश्चतुर्थस्थ खगा: भवेयुर्मंदगामिनः ।

रवे: पञ्चम षष्ठस्थाः भवेयुर्वंक्रगास्सदा ॥ १३ ॥

Stanza 13.—Planets in the 4th from the Sun possess slow motion ; those in the 5th and the 6th have somewhat retrograde motion.

रवेस्सप्तमरन्ध्रस्थ ग्रहश्चाल्येत वक्रगा: ।

रवेसुधर्मकंमस्थ ग्रहाणां कुटिलागतिः ॥ १४ ॥

Stanza 14.—Planets in the 7th and the 8th from the Sun possess retrograde motion; those in the 9th and the 10th from the Sun will have transverse motion.

रवेर्लाभ व्ययस्थाश्च ग्रहश्चात्यन्त शीघ्रगाः ।

शुभग्रहाणां शीघ्रगतयो बलहीनदाः ॥ १५ ॥

Stanza 15.—Planets in the 11th and the 12th from the Sun possess very swift motion. Swift motion renders benefics devoid of strength.

क्रूरग्रहाणां वक्रगतयइशुभमर्योंगदाः ।

इत्येवं हि ग्रहगतीर्दृष्टव्या गणिकोत्तमैः ॥ १६ ॥

Stanza 16.—Malefics cause good by having retrograde motion. In this way should be ascertained the movements of planets, by the learned in mathematics.

NOTES

In the last five stanzas the author introduces some astronomical elements. For astrological purposes they could be
taken to mean that planets, when situated at certain distances
from the Sun become strong or weak and thereby capable of
producing certain good or bad results.

In other words, the above means that all planets produce
ordinary results in the 3rd, 5th, 9th and 10th places from the
Sun. Malefics and benefics produce favourable and adverse
results respectively in 2, 5, 6, 7, 8, 11 and 12th places from
the Sun. This is of course the interpretation I have put. The
author has briefly suggested the different kinds of motions of
the planets and how they are beneficial or otherwise. According to *Suryasiddhanta* the motion of a planet is of eight kinds,
viz., Vakra (somewhat retrograde), *Ativakra* (retrograde),
Kutila (transverse), *Manda* (slow), *Atimanda* (very slow),
Sama (even), *Seeghra* (swift), and *Atiseeghra* (very swift).
We do not know the precise difference between the various
kinds of motion as they have not been elaborated. Our author
mentions all the above kinds of motion excepting *Atimanda*
(very slow). *Kutila* is held by some as a form of retrograde
motion. According to others, it is used to designate the
motion of a planet when being for the moment stationary in
respect to longitude and accordingly neither advancing no
retrograding, it is changing its latitude. The reader need not
have to worry with these highly technical points which are of
purely astronomical interest.

Thus ends the Thirteenth Chapter entitled "Malika Yoga"
in BHAVARTHA RATNAKARA of Sri Ramanujacharya.

CHAPTER XIV

अथ ग्रहाणां स्वक्षेत्रादि विचार तरङ्ग:

PLANETARY RULERSHIPS, ETC.

THE SUN—अथ रवे:

उच्चस्थानं रवेर्मेषं वृषमे तु द्विपद्‌गृहम् ।
मिथुनं तु समक्षेलं मिखक्षेलकुलीरकम् ॥ १ ॥

Stanza 1.—Aries is the place of exaltation for the Sun, Taurus is an inimical sign, Gemini is neutral, Cancer is friendly.

स्वक्षेलं मूलकोणं च सिंहप्रोक्तस्तु सूरिमि: ।
कन्याभं तु समक्षेलं तुलानीचारि मन्दिरम् ॥ २ ॥

Stanza 2.—For the Sun, Leo is Moolatrikona and own house, Virgo is neutral and Libra is the place of debilitation.

मिलक्षेले कीटधनुषी मकरं स्याद्विद्षद्‌गृहम् ।
कुम्भोऽपि शत्रुक्षेलञ्च निलक्षेलस्तु मीनभम् ।
रवेर्गृहाणां गणनास्त्वेवं प्रोक्ताच सूरिमि: ॥ ३ ॥

Stanza 3.—Scorpio and Sagittarius are friendly signs, Capricorn and Aquarius are inimical and Pisces friendly. So has to be ascertained the Sun's relationship with the signs.

NOTES

In the concluding part of the work, the author deals with the elements of astrology. The friendly, neutral or inimical nature of a sign for the Sun is based on the friendly, neutral or inimical nature of the disposition of its lord. Thus as Venus is an enemy of the Sun, Taurus is an inimical sign.

THE MOON—अथ चन्द्रः

विधोरजा समक्षेलमुच्चस्थानं वृपस्तथा ।
मूलकोण तथा प्रोक्तं मिवक्षेलं तु युभगमम् ॥ ४ ॥

Stanza 4.—For the Moon Aries is neutral, Taurus is the place of exaltation, the same is also Moolatrikona and Gemini is a neutral sign.

ककटं तु स्वभवनं मिलक्षेलं तु सिंहभं ।
कन्यामि तस्य भवनं तुला समगृहं भवेत् ॥ ५ ॥

Stanza 5.—Cancer is the own house, Leo and Virgo are friendly signs and Libra is neutral.

वृश्रिकं तु समक्षेलं नीचराशिरपिस्मृता ।
शरासनम् समगृहं मकरस्समगृहं भवेत् ॥ ६ ॥

Stanza 6.—Scorpio is the place of debilitation as well as a neutral sign and Sagittarius and Capricorn are neutral.

कुम्भक्षे तु समक्षेलं मीनस्यत्सम मन्दिरम् ।
विधोग्रहाणां गणनात्वेवं प्रोक्ताच सूरिभिः ॥ ७ ॥

Stanza   7.—Aquarius and Pisces are neutral. So
have said the learned in astrology as regards the
Moon's relationship with the signs.

MARS—अथ कुज:

कुजस्य मेषं स्वक्षेलं मूलकोणं तथैव च ।
वृषभं शुक्रभवनं मिथुनंत्वरिमन्दिरम् ॥ ८ ॥

Stanza   8.—For Mars, Aries is both own house
and Moolatrikona ; Taurus and Gemini are inimical.

कर्कटं नीचराशिश्च मित्रक्षेवदाहृतम् ।
सिंहर्क्षे मित्रभवनम् कन्या शत्रुगृहं भवेत् ॥ ९ ॥

Stanza   9.—Cancer is the place of debilitation
and a friendly sign ; Leo is friendly and Virgo is
inimical.

तुला शत्रुगृहं प्रोक्तं वृश्चिक स्वगृहं भवेत् ।
धनुर्मित्रगृहं प्रोक्तं मकरं शत्रुमन्दिरम् ॥ १० ॥

Stanza   10.—Libra is inimical. Scorpio is his own
sign, Sagittarius is friendly and Capricorn is inimical.

मकरंचोच्च राशिस्यत्कुम्भशत्रु गृहं भवेत् ।
मीने तु मित्रक्षेलस्यात्कुजस्येवं वदन्ति: ॥ ११ ॥

Stanza   11.—And Capricorn is the place of exaltation. Aquarius is inimical and Pisces is friendly. So
has been said for Mars.

MERCURY—अथ बुध:

बुधस्यजा समक्षेलं वृषोमित्रगृहं भवेत् ।
मिथुन स्वगृहं प्रोक्तं कर्कटं तु द्विषद् गृहं ॥ १२ ॥

Stanza 12.—For Mercury, Aries is a neutral sign, **Taurus** is friendly, Gemini is own house and Cancer is inimical.

सिंहर्क्षे मिलभावन कन्वा स्वलेलमुच्यते ।
मूलकोणंतुच्चराशि: कन्या सौमस्ययोगदा ॥ १३ ॥

Stanza 13.—Leo is friendly, Virgo is own house, Moolatrikona and place of exaltation.

तुलामिलगृहं प्रोक्तं वृश्चिकं समसन्दिरम् ।
धनुर्मृगौ समझेलं कुम्भर्क्षे समसन्दिरम् ॥ १४ ॥

Stanza 14.—Libra is friendly, and Scorpio, Sagittarius, Capricorn and Aquarius are neutral ones.

मीने समगृहं प्रोक्तं नीचराशिस्तथा भवेत् ।
बुधस्य गृह्राणानाःखेवं प्रोक्ता तु सूरिमि: ॥ १५ ॥

Stanza 15.—Pisces is neutral and place of debilitation. So have the learned in astrology assigned Mercury's relationship with signs.

JUPITER—अथ गुरु:

गुरोर्मेषं मिलगृहं वृषभमन्चरिमन्दिरम् ।
मिथुने शत्रृभवनमुच्चस्थानं तु कर्कटम् ॥ १६ ॥

Stanza 16.—For Jupiter, Aries is friendly, Taurus and Gemini are inimical and Cancer is the place of exaltation.

तदेव मिलभवनं िसिंहमं मिलमन्दिरम् ।
कन्या तुले शत्रृगृहे वृश्चिकं मिलमंदिरम् ॥ १७ ॥

Stanza 17.—Cancer and Leo are friendly, Virgo and Libra are inimical and Scorpio is friendly.

धनुस्थानं मूलकोणं स्वक्षेत्रचामिषीयते ।
मकरं नीचराशीतिस्वक्षेत्रमुदाहृतम् ॥ १८ ॥

Stanza 18.—Sagittarius is Moolatrikona and own house, Capricorn is the place of debilitation, and is also neutral.

कुम्भराशि समक्षेत्रं मीनं स्वभवनं भवेत् ।
गुरौ गृहाणां गणनात्वेवं प्रोक्तां तृ सूरिभिः ॥ १९ ॥

Stanza 19.—Aquarius is neutral and Pisces is own house. So have said the learned in astrology.

VENUS—अथ शुक्रः

भृगोर्मेषं समक्षेत्रं वृषभं स्वस्य मन्दिरम् ।
मिथुनं मित्रभवनं कर्कट त्वरिमन्दिरम् ॥ २० ॥

Stanza 20.—For Venus, Aries is neutral, Taurus is own house, Gemini is neutral and Cancer is inimical.

सिंहक्षे शत्रृभवनं कन्यानीचा सुहृद्गृहम् ।
स्वक्षेत्रं मूलकोणं च तुलाप्रोक्ता भृगुस्तथा ॥ २१ ॥

Stanza 21.—Leo is enemy's sign, Virgo is friendly and place of debilitation, and Libra is Moolatrikona and own house.

वृश्चिकं तु समक्षेत्रं धनुस्तवरिगृहं भवेत् ।
मकरं मित्रभवनं कुम्भस्तु सुहृदो गृहम् ॥ २२ ॥

Stanza 22.—Scorpio is neutral, Sagittarius is inimical and Capricorn and Aquarius are friendly.

मिनर्क्ष तु राशिस्यच्छतृक्षेत्र तथैव च ।

भृगोर्गृहाणां गणनात्वेवं प्रोक्ता च सूरिभि: ॥ २३ ॥

Stanza   23. - Pisces is the sign of exaltation and
is also inimical. So have the learned in astrology said
about Venus' relationship with the different signs.

SATURN—अथ शनि:

शनेर्मेषो नीचराशि शतृ क्षेत्रेमुदाहृतम् ।

वृषभं मिथुने चैव मित्रक्षेत्रसुदाहृतम् ॥ २४ ॥

Stanza   24.—For Saturn, Aries is the sign of
debility and an inimical place. Taurus and Gemini are
friendly.

कर्कटं शतृभवनं सिंहक्षं शतृमन्दिरम् ।

कन्यामित्र ग्रहंतौ ळितूच्चराशि सुहद्गृहम् ॥ २५ ॥

Stanza   25.—Cancer is inimical as also Leo.
Virgo is friendly and Libra is friendly as well as the
sign of exaltation.

वृश्चिकं शतृभवनं धनुस्समगृहं भवेत् ।

मकरं स्वभवनं कुम्भा स्वागारं मूलकोणकम् ॥ २६ ॥

Stanza   26.—Scorpio is inimical, Sagittarius is
neutral, Capricorn is own house, Aquarius is Moolatrikona, as well as own house.

मीनक्षेत्र समक्षेत्र मित्र्येव गृह निर्णय: ॥ २७ ॥

Stanza   27.—Pisces is a neutral sign. So are the
various signs disposed.

RAHU—अथ राहुः

वृषभौतुच्चराशिराहोः प्रोक्ते तु सूरिभिः ।
मिथुनं कर्कटं चैव मूलकोणमितिश्रुतम् ॥ २८ ॥

Stanza 28.—For Rahu, Taurus is the place of exaltation, Gemini and Cancer are Moolatrikonas.

मेषभं मित्रभवनं कन्या स्वभवनं भवेत् ।
उच्चस्थानस्थ राहोस्तु दायकालो हि राजदः ॥ २९ ॥

Stanza 29.—Aries is friendly and Virgo is own house. Rahu when exalted gives political power and fame in his Dasa.

KETU—अथ केतोः

केतो स्वभवनं मीनतुलामित्रस्य मन्दिरम् ।
कुम्भकीटैतुच्चराशि मूलकोणो धनुमृगौ ॥ ३० ॥

Stanza 30.—For Ketu, Pisces is own house, Libra is friendly, Aquarius is own house, Scorpio is the place of exaltation and Sagittarius and Capricorn are Moolatrikona places.

NOTES

The stanzas are simple and can be easily understood and therefore I have given no explanations. The author has assigned friendly places for Rahu and Ketu. Ketu is given ownership over two signs and two signs are also given for Moolatrikona. Similarly two sings are given for Moolatrikona for Rahu.

CONCLUSION

I have endeavoured to make the translation as simple and complete as possible. I am sure that after a careful perusal of the translation and the notes my esteemed readers will be highly benefited. The translation was concluded on Friday the 10th September 1943 at 8 p.m. (New I.S.T.) at Bangalore when the planetary positions were as follows :

Ascdt.		Mars	Sat.			Mars	Mercury
			Rahu Jupit.				Rahu
	RASI		Sun Venus	Jupit. Moon Ketu	NAVAMSA		
Ketu Moon							
			Merc.		Sun Saturn		Venus Ascdt.

A careful consideration of the above chart should suggest that the book will have a very good reception in the hands of the public especially because Lagnadhipati and Mercury are exalted and the Sun and Venus are in the 6th, Ketu in the 11th and Mars in the 3rd.

Index of Technical Terms

Alankara	—	Prosody.
Alpayu	—	Short Life.
Amla	—	Sour Taste.
Angas	—	Limbs, Parts.
Apoklimas	—	Succeedent houses.
Arishta	—	Misfortune.
Ayurbhava	—	8th house.
Ayushkaraka	—	Indicator of Longevity.
Badarayana	—	Vyasa, the famous Maharshi.
Balarishta	—	Infant Mortality.
Bhava	—	House.
Bhagya Yoga	—	Fortunate combination.
Bhagyavahana Yoga	—	Combinations bringing paraphernalia and vehicles.
Bhratru Bhava	—	3rd house.
Bhratrukaraka	—	Indicator of brothers, Mars.
Bhukti	—	Sub-period.
Brahma	—	Creator, the first of the Hindu Trinity.
Brahma Sutras	—	Philosophical aphorisms, composed by Vyasa.
Brihat Jataka	—	Famous work on Asrrology by Varahamihira.
Brihat Jataka Yoga	—	A Yoga mentioned in *Brihat Jataka*.
Budha	—	Mercury.

Budha Dasa	—	Period of Mercury.
Chandra	—	The Moon.
Chandra Dasa	—	The period of the Moon.
Chandra Mangala Yoga	—	Moon–Mars conjunction or mutual aspect.
Chandas	—	Rhetoric.
Dasa	—	Period.
Dasa Chidra	—	The end of a Dasa.
Dhana Bhava	—	2nd house.
Dhana Yoga	—	Combination for wealth.
Dhanur Lagna	—	Sagittarius rising.
Dharma Karmadhipa Yoga	—	Conjunction between 9th and 10th lord.
Dwirdwadasa	—	Planets disposed in the 2nd and 12th from each other.
Gajakesari Yoga	—	Mutual disposition of the Moon and Jupiter in quadrants.
Grandi Roga	—	A disease considered as fatal.
Guru Dasa	—	The period of Jupiter.
Gnana	—	Knowledge.
Guru-Chandala Yoga	—	Jupiter–Rahu conjunction.
Guru Mangala Yoga	—	Conjunction of Jupiter and Mars.
Jatakachandrika	—	An astrological treatise.
Jyotisha	—	Astrology
Kalathra Bhava	—	7th House.
Kanya Lagna	—	Virgo rising.
Karaka	—	Indicator.
Karma	—	Action, Profession.
Karma Bhava	—	10th House.
Karma Karaka	—	Jupiter.
Karkataka	—	Cancer.

Kashaya	—	Mixed taste.
Kavya	—	Poetry.
Kendra Yoga	—	A kind of Yoga.
Kendra	—	Quadrant.
Kendradhipathi	—	Lord of a quadrant.
Keraleeya	—	An ancient astrological treatise.
Ketu	—	Dragon's Tail.
Khahi	—	Astringent.
Khara	—	Hot.
Kuja	—	Mars.
Kumbha	—	Aquarius.
Kutumba	—	Family.
Labha Bhava	—	11th house.
Lagna	—	Ascendant.
Lagna Yoga	—	A combination formed by the position of planets in the Ascendant.
Lagnadhipathi	—	Lord of Ascendant.
Lavana	—	Saltish.
Lomasa	—	An ancient Indian astronomer.
Madhuram	—	Sweet.
Madhyayus	—	Middle Age.
Maharaja	—	A King or Ruler.
Maharaja Yogas	—	Combinations for Royalty.
Maharishi	—	A great sage.
Makara	—	Capricorn.
Maraka	—	Death or death inflicting.
Matru Bhava	—	4th house.
Mesha Lagna	—	Aries rising as Ascendant.
Misram	—	Mixed.
Mithuna	—	Gemini.

Moksha	—	Emancipation.
Moolatrikona	—	Position similar to exaltation.
Mrityu Karaka	—	Indicator of death.
Navamsa	—	1/9th Division of a sign.
Neecha	—	Debilitation.
Neecha Bhanga Raja Yoga	—	A combination paliating the debilitation.
Nirdhana Yoga	—	Combination for poverty.
Nirukta	—	A treatise expounding how Vedas are to be interpreted. Supposed to he composed by Rishi Yaska.
Panaparas	—	Succeedent Houses.
Parasara	—	A great sage and astrologer of Ancient India.
Parivarthana Yoga	—	Exchange of house or signs.
Pitru Bhava	—	9th House.
Pitrukaraka	—	The Sun.
Poornayus	—	Full Life.
Prakrithi	—	Nature.
Puranic	—	Stories of great heroes of Ancient India.
Rahu	—	Dragon's Head or Caput.
Rajasa	—	Virtues of "Nobility"— "Royalty".
Rasas	—	Tastes.
Sani	—	Saturn.
Sani Bhukti	—	Sub-period of Saturn.
Sankya Yogas	—	Certain combinations technically known as numerical Yogas.
Sarvartha Chintamani	—	A famous work on astrology.
Satkarma	—	Good actions or deeds.

Satru Bhava	—	6th House.
Satwikaguna	—	Pious nature
Simha Lagna	—	Leo as ascendant.
Sri Rama	—	The Hero of Ramayana.
Subha	—	Good, benefic.
Subha Parivarthana	—	Auspicious exchange of places.
Sudra	—	The 4th caste in Hinduism
Sukra Dasa	—	Period of Venus.
Tharka	—	Logic.
Thamas	—	Evil Nature.
Thanu Bhava	—	1st House.
Thanukaraka	—	Sun.
Thrikona	—	Trine.
Thrikonadhipathi	—	Lord of a Trine.
Thula Lagna	—	Libra as ascendant.
Upachayas	—	3rd, 6th, 10th, & 11th houses
Upa Veda	—	Treatise based on Vedas, e.g., Astrology, Ayurveda
Vahana	—	Vehicle. Conveyance.
Vahanakaraka	—	Venus.
Vahanasthana	—	4th House.
Vedas	—	Ancient Learning considered as Divine Revelations.
Vedangas	—	Limbs of the Vedas, e.g., Astrology, Grammar, etc.
Vedanta	—	A class of philosophy
Vidya	—	Knowledge, Learning.
Vimshottari	—	A Dasa based on constellations.
Vishnu	—	The second God amongst the Hindu Trinity.
Vrischika Lagna	—	Scorpio as ascendant.

Vrishabha Lagna	—	Taurus as ascendant.
Vyaya Bhava	—	12th House.
Yoga	—	(1) A particular combination of planets and signs.
		(2) Benefic results.
Yogakaraka	—	Planet giving rise to a special combination.